# Sea Monkeys and Brine Shrimp

By David Franklin

**Published by Adhurst Publishing Ltd. 2014**

**Copyright and Trademarks.** This publication is Copyright 2014 by Adhurst Publishing. All products, publications, software and services mentioned and recommended in this publication are protected by trademarks. In such instances, all trademarks & copyright belong to the respective owners.
All rights reserved. No part of this book may be reproduced or transferred in any form or by any means, graphic, electronic, or mechanical, including photocopying, recording, taping, or by any information storage retrieval system, without the written permission of the author. Pictures used in this book are either royalty free pictures bought from stock-photo websites or have the source mentioned underneath the photo.

**Disclaimer and Legal Notice.** This product does not offer legal or veterinary advice and should not be interpreted in that manner. The reader needs to do their own due-diligence to determine if the content of this product is right for them. If readers have purchased Sea Monkeys or Brine Shrimp that come with instructions, those instructions should take precedent. The author and any affiliates of this product are not liable for any damages or losses associated with the content in this product. While every attempt has been made to verify the information shared in this publication, neither the author or the affiliates assume any responsibility for errors, omissions or contrary interpretation of the subject matter herein. Any perceived slights to any specific person(s) or organization(s) are purely unintentional.

We have no control over the nature, content and availability of the websites listed in this book. The inclusion of any website link does not necessarily imply a recommendation or endorse the views expressed within them. Adhurst Publishing LTD takes no responsibility for, and will not be liable for, the websites being temporarily unavailable or being removed from the Internet. The accuracy and completeness of information provided herein and opinions stated herein are not guaranteed or warranted to produce any particular results, and the advice and strategies contained herein may not be suitable for every individual. The author shall not be liable for any loss incurred as a consequence of the use and application, directly or indirectly, of any information presented in this work. This publication is designed to provide information in regard to the subject matter covered.

# Table of Contents

Chapter One: Introduction ........................................................... 9
    Useful Terms to Know ........................................................ 11
Chapter Two: Understanding Sea Monkeys ....................... 15
    1.) What Are Sea Monkeys? ................................................ 16
    2.) Cool Facts about Sea Monkeys .................................... 19
        a.) Strange Sea Monkey Questions ............................... 20
        b.) Summary of Facts .................................................... 23
    3.) How Long do Sea Monkeys Live? ................................ 24
    4.) Why Do Sea Monkeys Make Good Pets? ................... 25
    5.) Sea Monkeys in Space! .................................................. 27
    6.) Types of Sea Monkeys ................................................... 29
Chapter Three: All the Practical Stuff ..................................... 31
    1.) How Many Should You Buy? ........................................ 32
    2.) Can Brine Shrimp Be Kept with Other Pets? ............. 33
    3.) How Much do Brine Shrimp Cost? .............................. 34
        a.) Initial Costs .............................................................. 34
        b.) Ongoing Costs ......................................................... 38
    4.) Pros and Cons of Sea Monkeys ................................... 40
    5.) What Equipment will I Need? ....................................... 42
Chapter Four: Purchasing Sea Monkeys ................................ 47

1.) Where to Buy Sea Monkeys ........................................48
   a.) Buying in the U.S. ....................................................48
   b.) Buying in the U.K. ....................................................50
2.) Buying Live vs. Raising from Eggs ..........................52

Chapter Five: Caring for Sea Monkeys..........................55
   1.) Where Do They Live? ...............................................56
      a.) Choosing a Tank................................................56
      b.) Fun Decorations for Sea Monkey Tanks................57
      c.) Tank Maintenance .............................................59
      d.) Summary of Facts..............................................62
   2.) Feeding Your Sea Monkeys......................................63
      a.) What Do They Eat? ............................................63
      b.) How Do You Feed Them?..................................64
      c.) Making Sea Monkey Food at Home.....................65
      d.) Summary of Facts..............................................66

Chapter Six: Hatching and Breeding Sea Monkeys...........67
   1.) Hatching Sea Monkeys from Eggs............................68
   2.) Breeding Sea Monkeys.............................................72

Chapter Seven: Keeping Sea Monkeys Healthy ...............75
   1.) Do Brine Shrimp Get Sick? .......................................76
      a.) Common Brine Shrimp Illnesses.........................76

2.) Keeping Sea Monkeys Healthy ..................................................83

Chapter Eight: Sea Monkeys Care Sheet............................89

    1.) Basic Information .......................................................90

    2.) Habitat Set-Up Guide .................................................91

    3.) Nutritional Information ................................................91

    4.) Hatching .....................................................................92

Chapter Nine: Common Mistakes Owners Make ................93

    1.) Inadequate Aeration ...................................................94

    2.) Overcrowding/Small Tank ..........................................96

    3.) Fluctuating Water Parameters ...................................97

Chapter Ten: Frequently Asked Questions .........................99

Chapter Eleven: Relevant Websites..................................105

    1.) Food for Sea Monkeys..............................................106

    2.) Aquariums for Sea Monkeys....................................108

    3.) Health Info for Sea Monkeys....................................110

    4.) General Info for Sea Monkeys.................................112

Index ..................................................................................114

Photo Credits.....................................................................120

References ........................................................................123

## Foreword

In this book you will find the answers to all of your questions about Sea Monkeys, which are a type of brine shrimp, including information about hatching, raising, feeding, health care, breeding and more. By the time you finish this book you will be an expert on keeping Sea Monkeys as pets.

It is possible to buy Sea Monkeys either as pre-packaged all-inclusive kit, or to buy them as eggs (or even live) separately. If you have bought your Sea Monkeys as part of a kit that contains specific instructions you should use this guidebook as a supplement to those instructions and not as a replacement to them.

## Acknowledgements

I would like to extend my thanks to my family and friends for supporting me throughout this journey.

I'd also like to thank my youngest daughter, Eva, who inspired me to write this book. Her fascination with Sea Monkeys sparked my own and we enjoyed researching this book together.

## Chapter One: Introduction

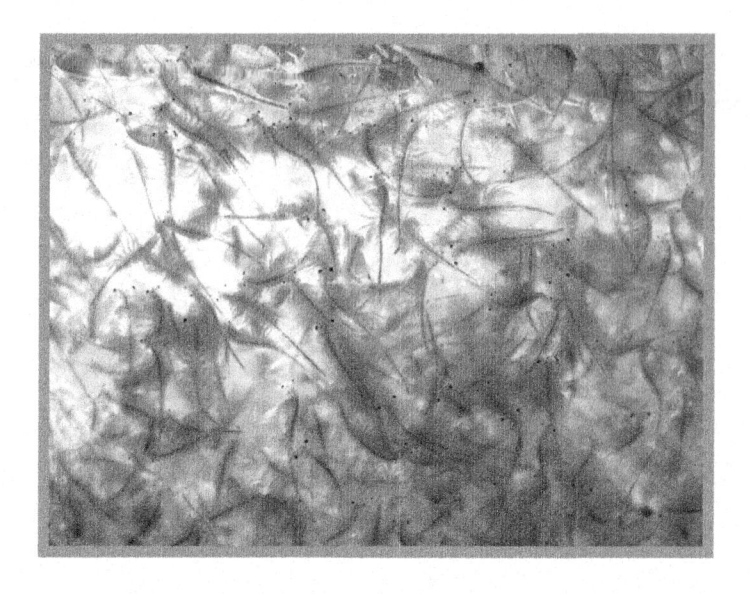

Sea Monkeys are small aquatic pets that can be raised from eggs and kept at home. These little creatures are actually a type of brine shrimp and they are often used as food for aquarium fish. When they are kept as pets, however, these animals are often referred to as Sea Monkeys, named for their monkey-like tails. Though they may be small, Sea Monkeys are incredibly entertaining – and they are easy to keep. In this book the terms Sea Monkey and Brine Shrimp are used interchangeably.

Harold von Braunhut is credited with inventing Sea Monkeys in 1957 – around the same time that ant farms became popular as both toys and pets. Sea Monkeys were advertised in comic books with illustrations of monkey-like sea creatures, which drew the attention of millions. Even

## Chapter One: Introduction

after more than 50 years, Sea Monkeys continue to be popular pets for both children and adults.

If you are thinking about keeping brine shrimp as a pet, you have come to the right place. In this book you will find all the information you need to prepare for your brine shrimp to hatch and to care for them properly. Within the pages of this book you will learn all the basics as well as some cool facts about Sea Monkeys including where they live, what they eat and how to care for them when they get sick.

After reading this book you should be able to care for your own Sea Monkeys and also to help your friends if they want to keep them too. So don't wait any longer – start reading.

# Chapter One: Introduction

## Useful Terms to Know

**Aeration** – a process of moving air through an aquarium in order to help oxygenate the water

**Algae** – aquatic growths of plant-like organisms; can easy overpopulate the tank in an excess of light or nutrients

**Ammonia** – also known as NH3, a toxic substance that is the result of waste build-up in the aquarium

**Aquascape** – referring to the physical design and layout of an aquarium including plants and accessories

**Biological Filtration** – a filtration method carried out by beneficial bacteria, helping to maintain the nitrogen cycle

**Chemical Filtration** – a filtration method using chemical processes to remove dissolved wastes from tank water

**Chlorine** – a chemical used to purify tap water by killing bacteria; toxic to fish and must be removed from water before using in a tank

**Cycling** – another word for establishing the nitrogen cycle in the tank; refers to establishing a colony of beneficial bacteria in the tank

## Chapter One: Introduction

**Denitrification** – the process by which anaerobic bacteria convert nitrate into nitrogen gas that is then released from the aquarium

**Hydrometer** – a device used to measure the specific gravity of salt water – i.e. what the concentration of salt is in your tank

**Mechanical Filtration** – a type of filtration that involves the physical removal of solid wastes from tank water

**Nauplii** – refers to the larvae of copepods (plural); newly hatched brine shrimp

**Nitrate** – also known as NO3, the final product in the nitrogen cycle; can be dangerous at high levels

**Nitrite** – also known as NO2, the second product in the nitrogen cycle; highly toxic to aquatic life

**Nitrogen Cycle** – the process through which wastes are broken down in the tank by bacteria, converting ammonia into nitrite and then into nitrate

**pH** – a measure of the concentration of hydrogen and hydroxide atoms in water; measured on a scale of 0 to 14

**Salinity** – a measure of the amount of salt in sea water; typically measured in parts per thousand (ppt)

## Chapter One: Introduction

**Sponge Filter** – a type of mechanical/biological filter in which water passes through a sponge before being returned to the tank

**Water Change** – the process of replacing a portion of tank water with clean water

# Chapter Two: Understanding Sea Monkeys

You may already have a basic idea about what Sea Monkeys and brine shrimp are and what they are like as pets, but there is much more to know. In this chapter you will learn details about what kind of animal brine shrimp are as well as information about their anatomy and biology. You will also learn some cool facts about Sea Monkeys including information about Sea Monkeys in space! After reading this chapter you will have enough information to properly consider whether they are the right choice as a pet for you.

## Chapter Two: Understanding Sea Monkeys

### 1.) What Are Sea Monkeys?

The term "Sea Monkey" refers not to a specific species of animal, but rather the brand name for type of brine shrimp sold as novelty aquarium pets. As mentioned in the introduction, Harold von Braunhut coined the brand name Sea Monkeys in 1962, though the product was originally released in 1957 under a different name.

Brine shrimp are a type of aquatic crustacean belonging to the genus Artemia, the only genus in the family Artemiidae.

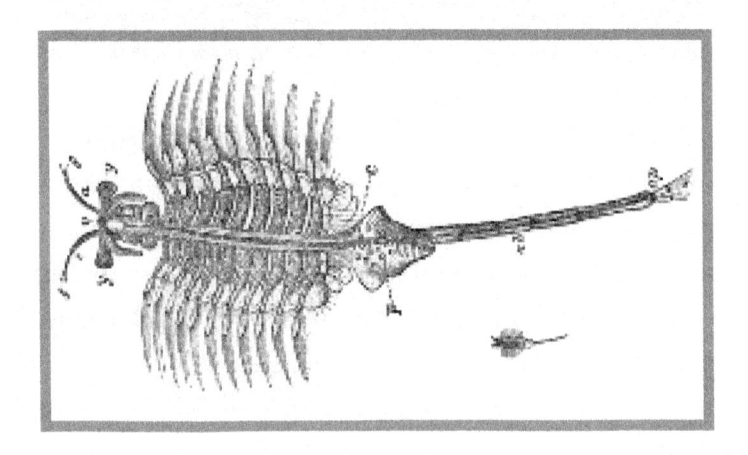

The word "genus" is used to group animals by their genetic similarities – it is a term used by scientists and researchers. Brine shrimp have existed for many years, since the

## Chapter Two: Understanding Sea Monkeys

Triassic period, and the earliest evidence of their existence dates back to 982. Brine shrimp are found in bodies of saltwater throughout the world, but not in the ocean – they are typically found in inland saltwater lakes. What enables these tiny crustaceans to survive is the fact that they can withstand salinity levels between 25% and 250%, thus ensuring that they do not often cohabitate with predators like fish.

Because the term "brine shrimp" applies to a genus of animals rather than one in particular, there are actually several species of brine shrimp. The genus Artemia contains different species, all of which are thought to have diverged from a single species living in the Mediterranean Sea over 5 million years ago.

Technically, brine shrimp are a type of arthropod, having a segmented body to which leaf-like appendages are attached. Though the specifics vary from one species to another, they generally have 19 body segments, 11 of which have attached appendages. The next two segments are fused, housing the reproductive organs, and the final segments lead to the tail.

The average length of a Sea Monkey is between 8 and 10mm (0.31 to 0.39 in) for an adult male and between 10 and 12mm (0.39 to 0.47 in) for a female. The width of both sexes is similar, about 4mm (0.16 in). Though the body of brine shrimp has a number of segments, it is generally divided into three parts: the head, thorax and abdomen. The whole body is protected by a thin exoskeleton (hard coating on the outside of the body) made up of a fibrous substance called chitin. This exoskeleton sheds periodically and, in females, this shedding precedes the period during which female Sea Monkeys become ready to ovulate (produce eggs).

## Chapter Two: Understanding Sea Monkeys

### 2.) Cool Facts about Sea Monkeys

Brine shrimp, or Sea Monkeys, are very interesting creatures. From afar they look like tiny insects swimming around but, up close, they are complex organisms that have developed a number of unique adaptations. The three main functions of brine shrimp include digestion, swimming and reproduction. Interestingly, however, these functions are not controlled by the brain. Rather, brine shrimp have a complex nervous system that controls and regulates these functions. This nervous system also enables the brine shrimp to voluntarily drop parts of the body in defense.

The eyes of brine shrimp are also very unique – they actually have two different types of eyes. Brine shrimp have two compound eyes that are attached to flexible stalks – these eyes serve as the main optical sense organ for adults of the species. In juveniles, or nauplii, there is a naupliar eye which is situated in the center of the head. This eye is the only functional optical sense organ in nauplii and it loses function once the brine shrimp reach adulthood.

It has already been mentioned that brine shrimp can withstand extremely high salinity levels (25% to 250%). To get an idea what this means, consider the fact that the salinity of the ocean is about 3.5% on average. Brine shrimp are very small creatures and they are often used as live food in the aquarium industry. In the wild, however, their ability to withstand high salinity levels ensures that they typically do not coexist with fish and other predators. In fact,

## Chapter Two: Understanding Sea Monkeys

brine shrimp are most commonly found in natural habitats with salinity levels of 60 to 80%.

The reproduction methods of brine shrimp are also very interesting. Males of the species are anatomically different from females in that they have an enlarged second antenna. These antennae are modified into claw-like organs that can grip objects – these organs are used in the mating process. An adult female brine shrimp is capable of ovulating every 140 hours and, in ideal conditions, the eggs may hatch almost immediately after being laid. When conditions are not ideal, however, the female may produce eggs with a chorion coating. This coating renders the eggs metabolically inactive (they do not die but do not grow) and they can remain dormant for up to 10 years in a dry, oxygen-free (anaerobic) environment.

Another fascinating fact about brine shrimp is that they breathe through little gill plates in their feet!

### a.) Strange Sea Monkey Questions

When you are learning about something new, everything is fair game. There are certain topics which can seem silly, however, and that is definitely the case with brine shrimp. Below you will find some strange questions that often get asked about Sea Monkeys as well as their answers.

**Q**: Do Sea Monkeys really look like little monkeys?

## Chapter Two: Understanding Sea Monkeys

**A**: While Sea Monkeys don't have fur and they don't make the typical monkey noises, they do have long tails and they can move very quickly. You shouldn't expect them to look like little underwater monkeys but they are active and playful like monkeys.

**Q**: Do brine shrimp bite?
**A**: Brine shrimp are too small for you to actually pick them up and hold them, so there shouldn't be any occasion where they would even be able to bite you. If you stick your hand in the tank, however, you may be able to touch them – just make sure your hands are clean and do not contain any soap residue. Sea Monkeys do not bite but you may find that if they swim around your hand that it tickles.

**Q**: Do Sea Monkeys really fall in love?
**A**: You may have heard about things like Sea Monkeys cuddling, kissing and falling in love. While they do not exhibit these actions in the same way that humans do, you may sometimes see your Sea Monkeys clinging to each other and they might start following each other around. This is part of their mating ritual and it could mean that you will soon have baby brine shrimp in your tank.

**Q**: Do Sea Monkeys change color?
**A**: Yes. Sea Monkeys can change color depending on what they eat or simply what they feel like doing. You may see your brine shrimp display a range of colors from white to dark red.

## Chapter Two: Understanding Sea Monkeys

**Q**: Can I train my Sea Monkeys?
**A**: While you can't necessarily train Sea Monkeys to do tricks like jumping through a hoop, you may find some of their natural tendencies amusing. For example, if you shine a small flashlight on one end of the aquarium, the Sea Monkeys will all flock to it – they may even follow it as you move it around the tank.

**Q**: What do I do if I go on vacation?
**A**: If you go on vacation see if you can get a friend to take care of them for you. If you are only leaving for a week, however, your Sea Monkeys should do just fine on their own.

**Q**: Do Sea Monkeys fight?
**A**: While it isn't usually a constant problem, your male Sea Monkeys may fight on occasion – you may find them interlocked but you shouldn't try to separate them because they could get hurt. Females, on the other hand, do not tend to fight with each other.

**Q**: Do Sea Monkeys like sunlight?
**A**: Yes, Sea Monkeys flock to natural light and it will also help to keep the water in their tank warm. Be careful about leaving them in direct sunlight, however, because it could make the tank water too warm and could cause some of it to evaporate too quickly. You should not allow the temperature to rise to more than 80°F or 26.6°C as this could be harmful or even fatal to them.

Chapter Two: Understanding Sea Monkeys

## b.) Summary of Facts

**Scientific Name**: genus Artemia, family Artemiidae
**Common Name**: brine shrimp
**Type of Animal**: aquatic crustacean
**Discovery**: historical records date back to 982
**Habitat:** inland saltwater lakes, worldwide
**Adaptations:** ability to withstand salinity of 25% to 250%
**Size (male):** 8 to 10 mm (0.31 to 0.39 in) long, 4 mm (0.16 in) wide
**Size (female):** 10 to 12 mm (0.39 to 0.47 in) long, 4 mm (0.16 in) wide
**Anatomy**: body has 19 segments; three sections including a tail and 2 eyes (in adults, 3 when young)
**Reproduction**: eggs; can lay dormant for years
**Ovulation**: every 140 hours
**Eggs**: may hatch immediately after laying; can lay dormant for up to 10 years in anaerobic conditions
**Common Use**: live food for fish and crustaceans, aquatic pets, biological research, etc.

## Chapter Two: Understanding Sea Monkeys

## 3.) How Long do Sea Monkeys Live?

The lifespan of Sea Monkeys is relatively short compared to other pets. It may also be highly variable, depending on the conditions in which they are kept. For example, if the temperature of the tank is not within the ideal range or if you do not provide an adequate or appropriate diet, these factors could drastically decrease the lifespan of your pets.

On average, the biological lifespan of a brine shrimp is about 1 to 2 years. This starts from the time they are hatched to the time they die. Because their lifespan is relatively short, brine shrimp grow and mature fairly quickly so that they are able to reproduce before they die. In fact, their eggs often hatch within a few hours of being laid.

## Chapter Two: Understanding Sea Monkeys

## 4.) Why Do Sea Monkeys Make Good Pets?

If you are looking for a pet that is entertaining to keep and easy to care for, Sea Monkeys are definitely one to consider. The fact that they are fun to watch and don't require a lot of care are just two of the reasons that make brine shrimp great pets, however. Below you will find a list of more reasons to consider these animals as a pet:

1. **They are inexpensive**. Not only is it cheap to buy a few brine shrimp eggs, but you can also get a small aquarium for a low price or just buy an all-inclusive Sea Monkey kit.

2. **They are easy to keep**. While many people think of a dog or cat when they think of having a pet, these animals can be difficult to take care of. Sea Monkeys, on the other hand, are very easy to care for – it is so easy nearly anyone can do it!

3. **Little cleaning is required**. All Sea Monkeys require is a partial water change now and then to keep the tank clean.

4. **They are self-perpetuating**. Sure, Sea Monkeys may only have a lifespan of about 1-2 years, but they breed readily so you will always have new Sea Monkeys in your tank. Even if you manage to kill the entire tank, you can dry it out then refill it to activate the dormant eggs your Sea Monkeys left behind.

## Chapter Two: Understanding Sea Monkeys

5. **They can be very educational**. Not only is the experience of owning and caring for a pet a great educational experience, but Sea Monkeys can also help to teach you about the cycle of life and reproduction. Watching a tiny speck of an egg develop into a living creature is a wonderful learning experience.

6. **They can help teach responsibility.** Whilst they are not high maintenance there are certain things you need to do to keep your brine shrimp happy and healthy and as a consequence they can be a good way to teach children about being responsible for another living creature.

7. **They can help you relax.** Purdue University in Indianna has carried out a few studies on filled aquariums and their effects over the years. Proven benefits include helping people to become calmer and less stressed and watching marine life in tanks has even been shown to stop babies crying!

Chapter Two: Understanding Sea Monkeys

## 5.) Sea Monkeys in Space!

In the early 1990s, Sea Monkeys made headlines as the first animal to be born in space. In April of 1991, forty-four brine shrimp hatched in the space shuttle Atlantis as part of a scientific experiment regarding the effects of microgravity on developing organisms. This study was conducted by biologists from Kansas State University and the University of Nebraska at Lincoln.

What made Sea Monkeys the ideal test subjects for this experiment was the fact that their birth and development can be completely controlled. Cysts, the dried eggs of brine shrimp, were taken into space and hatched aboard the shuttle once it was in orbit. The dried eggs were stored in syringes and then exposed to saltwater once the shuttle was in space. The exposure to seawater triggered the hatching of the eggs and started their development.

## Chapter Two: Understanding Sea Monkeys

The results of this study revealed that there were no significant changes in the number of brine shrimp that hatched from the eggs in space compared to the number that would likely have hatched on Earth. While only five of the brine shrimp were still living by the time the shuttle landed, it is thought that issues with oxygenation and insufficient nutrients in the water were more to blame for the death of the other brine shrimp than the zero-gravity conditions of space.

In addition to studying the birth and growth of animals in space, this brine shrimp study served an additional purpose. Scientists wanted to see if brine shrimp had the potential to become a link in the food chain for astronauts living in space stations. Waste produced by astronauts could be a food source for algae which, in turn, could become a food source for brine shrimp. The shrimp themselves could be eaten by the astronauts or used as food for fish that the astronauts could eat.

Chapter Two: Understanding Sea Monkeys

## 6.) Types of Sea Monkeys

As you have already learned, the term "Sea Monkey" is an alternative name for a breed of brine shrimp. Brine shrimp are not a particular species but rather a genus comprised of different species. The species of brine shrimp are:

- Artemia franciscana (San Francisco brine shrimp)
- Artemia gracilis (New England brine shrimp)
- Artemia monica (Mono brine shrimp)
- Artemia parthenogenetica
- Artemia persimilis
- Artemia salina
- Artemia sinica
- Artemia urmiana

Sea Monkeys are a type of Artemia Salina – in fact they are a hybrid type of brine shrimp known as Artemia NYOS (short for New York Ocean Science). This hybrid was created in an effort to make them more resilient as pets as they theoretically live longer and grow slightly larger.

The reason there are so many different types of brine shrimp may be linked to the fact that they are widely distributed throughout the world in a variety of isolated habitats. While it is thought that all the different species diverged from a single species over 5 million years ago, there now exist many different geographical strains. It is even possible for two different species to live within the same habitat.

Chapter Two: Understanding Sea Monkeys

What makes each species unique is its adaptations to the particular environment in which it lives. Some inland saltwater lakes have a higher concentration of salt, for example. Certain bodies of water have essentially the same salt concentration as seawater – an example of this type of water is the Great Salt Lake in Utah. Other types of water, on the other hand, have a different concentration of salt in the water with varying degrees of sulphate, carbonate and potassium.

# Chapter Three: All the Practical Stuff

Now that you know the facts about brine shrimp, you are ready to learn the practical bits. How many should you buy? And can they be kept with fish? In this chapter you will learn the answers to these questions and many more. By the time you get through this chapter you will have a better idea about the practical aspects of keeping Sea Monkeys or brine shrimp as pets. Once you do, you will be ready to move on to thinking about actually buying them.

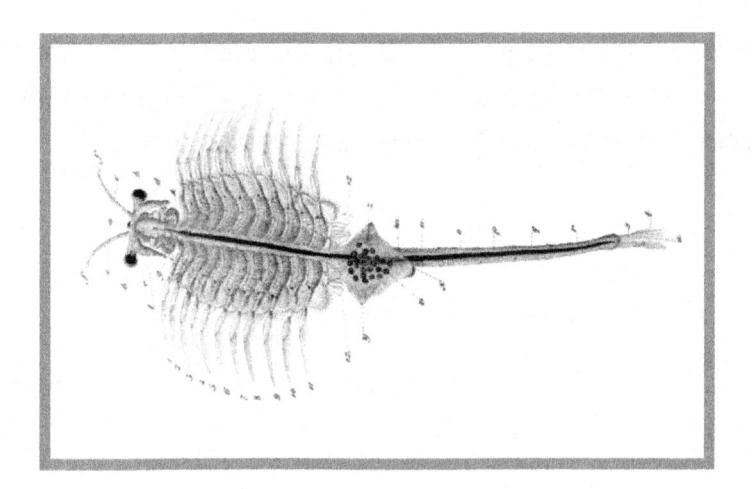

Chapter Three: All the Practical Stuff

## 1.) How Many Should You Buy?

One of the great benefits of brine shrimp is that they are very small – this means that you can usually keep a good number of them in the same tank.

Brine shrimp eggs are even smaller of course, so it is very difficult to count them. It's also hard to predict how many from a batch will actually hatch and then go on to breed successfully. As overcrowding can occasionally be an issue, it's best to start the hatching process with one batch or packet of brine shrimp or Sea Monkey eggs, and add to their numbers later when you can see how many are developing.

You may decide it's worth keeping an additional packet of eggs on standby in case only a few of the first packet hatch, or your pets don't successfully have babies quickly.

## Chapter Three: All the Practical Stuff

## 2.) Can Brine Shrimp Be Kept with Other Pets?

Because they are aquatic creatures, you may be tempted to think that brine shrimp can be kept in an aquarium with other animals like fish. In reality, however, brine shrimp are often used as live food for fish so, if you combine the two, the brine shrimp won't last long. You also have to consider the fact that brine shrimp tend to prefer environments with very high salinity levels – not many other organisms can survive in this type of environment.

For the wellbeing of your brine shrimp and Sea Monkeys, it is recommended that you keep them in a dedicated tank only with other brine shrimp.

## Chapter Three: All the Practical Stuff

## 3.) How Much do Brine Shrimp Cost?

As is true with any pet, you should have an idea how much the pet is going to cost you before you buy one. Unfortunately, many pet owners find that they do not have the financial ability to care for their pets after they have already bought them. The pet must then be passed off to another home where it may not get the care it deserves. To ensure that your Sea Monkeys get the best care possible, take the time to learn about their needs so you can be sure you will be able to care for them throughout the entire lives.

In this section you will find a detailed breakdown of the costs associated with keeping brine shrimp as pets. You will find descriptions of the initial costs you can expect when buying your Sea Monkeys or brine shrimp as well as the on-going costs for keeping them. Only if you can afford to cover all of these costs comfortably should you purchase them as pets.

### a.) Initial Costs

The initial costs include those costs which you must cover in order to buy the brine shrimp and to supply them with the proper environment. Some of these costs include the purchase price of the eggs, the cost for a tank or aquarium, tank decorations and other accessories like salt for the water and water purifier. Below you will find a detailed description of each cost as well as a price estimation.

## Chapter Three: All the Practical Stuff

**Purchase Price**: Brine shrimp eggs are very inexpensive and, because they are so small, you get a significant number of them in a small package. A packet of freeze-dried brine shrimp eggs should cost you no more than $5 or $10 (£3.25 - £6.50). A pre-packaged Sea Monkey kit will cost in the region of $10 - $20 (£6.50 - £16).

**Aquarium/Tank**: An aquarium or tank for your Sea Monkeys can be as simple or complex as you like. Some people raise them in something as simple as a plastic soda bottle. If you want something a little more exciting, however, you can purchase a basic aquarium tank which will also provide them with more room to swim around. In general, you shouldn't have to spend more than $20 (£13) for your Sea Monkey aquarium.

**Decorations**: The decorations for your tank depend greatly on the size and shape of your tank. If you have a small tank, for example, you may not have much room for decorations. The ideal decorations for a brine shrimp tank include fake plants, small rocks or shells and novelty aquarium decorations. You can expect to spend about $15 (£9.75) or less on decorations for your tank but of course if you choose to you can add more decorations later on.

**Equipment**: In order to keep your brine shrimp healthy, you need to maintain a certain temperature and salinity level in your tank. To measure the salinity, you may need to invest in a hydrometer. A hydrometer is a type of device that can

## Chapter Three: All the Practical Stuff

be used to measure the salt content of water. This device is made of glass and it is usually lowered into the water where it floats, giving a reading of the salt content.

To keep track of the temperature in your tank, you should invest in an aquarium thermometer. For small tanks, you are not likely to need an aquarium heater – in most cases, a lamp will keep the tank warm enough. For large tanks if you plan to have a very large number of brine shrimp, however, you might consider buying an aquarium heater and a sponge filter.

You will also need an air pump to increase circulation in the water, especially if you plan to hatch your brine shrimp or Sea Monkeys from eggs.

It's useful to get a magnifying glass so that you can examine your small pets in greater detail.

The cost for this equipment may range from $20 to $45 (£12 - £28).

**Accessories**: Sea Monkeys live in salt water, so you will need to keep a stock of non-iodized salt like synthetic sea salt on hand. You will also need to purchase some kind of water purifier like a dechlorination agent to remove toxins and chemicals from tap water before using it in your tank (you can use distilled or filtered water as a base instead of tap water and in fact if you are purchasing a pre-packaged kit the instructions will probably say that you should do so).

Chapter Three: All the Practical Stuff

These products should cost you between $10 and $15 (£6.50 - £9.75).

### Initial Costs for Sea Monkeys

| Cost Type | Price ($) | Price (£) |
|---|---|---|
| Purchase Price | $5 to $20 | £3.25 - £16 |
| Aquarium/Tank | $20 | £13 |
| Decorations | $15 | £9.75 |
| Equipment | $20 to $45 | £12 - £28 |
| Accessories | $10 to $15 | £6.50 - £9.75 |

Chapter Three: All the Practical Stuff

## b.) Ongoing Costs

The ongoing costs for keeping Sea Monkeys include costs for those things which you may need to buy every month or so. The most obvious ongoing cost is of course food but there may also be times when you need or want to buy additional supplies. Below you will find a detailed description of some of these as well as price estimations.

**Food**: Brine shrimp are very small, so they do not eat a significant amount of food. They subsist primarily on algae and phytoplankton which can be purchased in powdered form, specifically designed for brine shrimp. Algae is a type of aquatic organism made of tiny cells – it often resembles a plant. Phytoplankton are tiny cells which drift through the water in the ocean, providing food for many aquatic animals including Sea Monkeys. A small container of brine shrimp food should last you at least a month (some can last up to six months) and shouldn't cost more than $5 (£3.25).

**Extra Eggs**: Over the course of time, some of your Sea Monkeys will die. As long as you keep the conditions in your aquarium healthy, however, the number should be minimal. You may choose to occasionally hatch new Sea Monkeys to supplement the population in your tank, especially if you decided to start with a small quantity. An extra packet of brine shrimp eggs should be enough to supplement your tank for a few months and it shouldn't cost more than $5

## Chapter Three: All the Practical Stuff

(£3.25). Of course if you can breed your brine shrimp successfully you may not ever need to buy new eggs!

**Additional Supplies**: In addition to food and extra eggs, there are a few other supplies you might need from month to month in order to care for your Sea Monkeys. Some of the supplies you might need include extra water purifier, replacement decorations or repairs to the aquarium, replacement light bulbs, medicine etc. You may also want to purchase an aquarium water test kit so you can keep an eye on the water parameters in your tank. You shouldn't expect to spend more than $10 (£6.50) per month maximum on these costs and there should be many months when you don't need to purchase anything additional.

### Ongoing Costs for Sea Monkeys

| Cost Type | Price ($) | Price (£) |
| --- | --- | --- |
| Food | $5 | £3.25 |
| Extra Eggs (occasional cost only) | $5 | £3.25 |
| Additional Supplies | $10 | £6.50 |

Chapter Three: All the Practical Stuff

## 4.) Pros and Cons of Sea Monkeys

Before you go out and buy Sea Monkeys for yourself or your family, you should learn the pros and cons of these creatures as pets. Every pet has its advantages and disadvantages, and they are unique. Below you will find a list of both the pros and cons of brine shrimp so you can make an educated decision regarding whether they are the right pet for you.

**Pros for Sea Monkeys**

- Very inexpensive to buy and keep
- Entertaining – very active in the aquarium
- Easy to keep, require little upkeep and cleaning
- Can be kept in a variety of aquariums – can even buy an all-inclusive kit
- Educational – really great for teaching kids about the cycle of life
- Easy to raise from eggs at home – can also buy live
- Eggs hatch within 24 hours of exposure to salt water

**Cons for Sea Monkeys**

- Very small, may not be easy to see clearly
- Only have a lifespan of around 1-2 years

## Chapter Three: All the Practical Stuff

- Require salt water to live – which requires some preparation
- May require additional equipment like air pumps, lamps and thermometers
- Not all of the eggs will hatch each time

Chapter Three: All the Practical Stuff

## 5.) What Equipment will I Need?

While Sea Monkeys are easy pets to keep you may need to install some equipment in your tank to keep things running smoothly.

Below you will find an in-depth explanation of each of these pieces of equipment:

**Air Pump**

Water circulation is incredibly important in hatching brine shrimp eggs. The ideal solution is to install an air stone or some other type of bubble machinery in your brine shrimp hatchery. Not only will this device increase water movement in the tank, but it will also help to oxygenate the water. Without adequate oxygen and circulation, your Sea Monkey eggs may not hatch or develop properly.

**Aquarium Filter**

If you keep your Sea Monkeys in a small tank or a Sea Monkey kit, you are unlikely to need an aquarium filter. For larger tanks or large numbers of Sea Monkeys, however, you might want to consider an one. The best kind of filter for a Sea Monkey tank is a sponge filter because it provides both mechanical and biological filtration while posing little

## Chapter Three: All the Practical Stuff

danger to the Sea Monkeys. Mechanical filtration is simply the process of removing solid waste particles from tank water while biological filtration is the process of harboring beneficial bacteria which help to keep the tank water clean and clear.

When it comes to aquarium filters, you have be careful with certain models that have powerful suction – this includes power filters, canister filters and inline filters. With these filters there is a risk of your Sea Monkeys being sucked up the tube and into the filter. With a sponge filter, however, the sponge tempers the suction of the filter and the pores in the sponge should be small enough that your Sea Monkeys won't get caught anyway. This type of filter will also help to remove solid debris from the tank while encouraging the growth of a colony of beneficial bacteria.

Remember that unless you have a large tank of Sea Monkeys you don't need to need to worry about filters.

### Heater/Thermometer

Whatever your tank size, in order to keep your tank within the proper temperature range, it's very helpful to know what the water temperature in your tank is. Tank thermometers come in a variety of shapes and sizes – some you can stick directly to the wall of your tank and others you can drop in to the tank.

## Chapter Three: All the Practical Stuff

Once you know what the temperature in your Sea Monkey tank is, you can adjust it using either a lamp or, if your tank is larger and you wish to make the additional investment, an aquarium heater. When purchasing a heater, be sure to get one that is rated for the size tank you have – a heater that is too big may overheat your tank and kill all of your brine shrimp. Aquarium heaters should be used to stabilize and maintain tank water temperatures, not to make drastic changes.

**Hydrometer**

Whilst brine shrimp can withstand a wide range of salinity levels (25%-250%) that doesn't mean that they like or are able to cope with big variations or sudden drastic changes in salinity levels. The best range for them is between 30-35 ppt. In order to measure how salty your pets water is a crucial bit of kit is a hydrometer – which measures the specific gravity of the water.

There are different types of hydrometer on the market but most will involve you collecting a sample of water from the tank that the hydrometer will then measure for salinity levels. When purchasing a hydrometer make sure you're getting one that is sold specifically for aquarium use. Normally when you need to just top up water in your tank a little bit due to some of the water evaporating you would not need to use salt water but instead top it up with either distilled or bottled water. This is because when the water evaporates the water in the tank becomes slightly more salty as the salt is not evaporating at the same rate as the water. When you're performing a partial water change, however, and changing around 25% of the water you would normally need to use saline or salty water.

The hydrometer is a fantastic tool because it allows you to double check before adding any water to the tank what the current salinity levels are. You can then adjust the water you're adding to the tank to either make the water more or less saline. So for example, if the water in the tank has become too salty due to water evaporation you know just to top up with bottled or treated water but if for any reason the salinity level has dropped below 30 ppt you know you'll need to add a small amount of salt to the treated water you're adding to bring the salinity levels back up.

## Tank Lighting

Lighting is not a necessity for keeping Sea Monkeys, but it will make them more visible for you to enjoy them. If you do not have a heater installed in your tank, a basic incandescent or grow lamp will help to keep the tank warm.

You should be careful, however, when using a lamp in your brine shrimp tank because you do not want to overheat the water. The ideal temperature range for a Sea Monkey tank is between 70 and 80°F (21 to 26.6°C), though hatching temperatures are ideally at the top end of this scale. You

## Chapter Three: All the Practical Stuff

should make sure that the temperature doesn't fall below 60°F (15.5°C) or rise above 80°F (26.6°C) as this can be harmful or even fatal to Sea Monkeys.

Sea Monkeys love sunlight and this can also help heat the tank water. It is always best to position the tank in indirect sunlight though, and to keep an eye on the temperature if it is particularly hot, as it's important the water temperature doesn't rise too much.

# Chapter Four: Purchasing Sea Monkeys

If you have decided that Sea Monkeys are the right pet for you and your family, you have come to the right place. Now that you know the basics about them, you are ready to move on to learning where to buy them. In this chapter you will learn where you can find brine shrimp and Sea Monkeys and what you should know before you decide where to get them.

Purchasing your brine shrimp or Sea Monkeys from a reputable supplier is the first step in helping to assure that your new pets are happy and healthy during their life with you.

# Chapter Four: Purchasing Sea Monkeys

## 1.) Where to Buy Sea Monkeys

Since they were first introduced in the 1950s, Sea Monkeys have been fairly easy to find. They were originally advertised in the back of comic books, but now you can find them at local pet stores, online and even in toy stores around the world. Before you go out and buy Sea Monkeys, take the time to consider your options so you don't end up buying eggs that never hatch or an aquarium that doesn't suit your new pets. In this section you will learn about some of the best options for buying Sea Monkeys in both the U.S. and the U.K.

### a.) Buying in the U.S.

To find brine shrimp, all you have to do is visit the aquarium aisle at your local pet store. Most pet stores, even small stores, typically have freeze-dried brine shrimp eggs (cysts) for sale. If you ask, you may also be able to order larger quantities of them if you plan to cultivate a large colony of brine shrimp. If you are looking for novelty Sea Monkey kits that come with the eggs as well as an aquarium, you might want to look online or check your local toy store. In the United States, chains like Toys R Us and Amazon sell Sea Monkey kits in stores and online, so look around.

One thing to be aware of when purchasing brine shrimp is that the eggs come in two forms – decapsulated or encapsulated. Encapsulated cysts have a sort of shell that

## Chapter Four: Purchasing Sea Monkeys

keeps the egg protected and dormant until it is exposed to saltwater. These eggs may take longer to hatch and they leave behind a shell. Decapsulated eggs have already had the shells removed so it takes less time and energy to hatch these eggs.

If you decide to purchase a pre-packaged or all-inclusive Sea Monkey kit please do make sure that you read ALL of the instructions it contains very carefully. There are some instances where you may need to follow different instructions to those in this book, for example when hatching your Sea Monkeys where you will most likely be provided with a unique 'water purifier'.

To buy brine shrimp eggs try these suppliers:

Brine Shrimp Direct. <http://www.brineshirmpdirect.com>

Doctors Foster and Smith. <http://www.drsfostersmith.com>

Sea-Monkey.com. <http://www.sea-monkey.com/>

You can also buy live brine shrimp online:

LiveAquariua.com. <http://www.liveaquaria.com>

LiveBrineShrimp.com. <http://www.livebrineshrimp.com/>

Blue Zoo Aquatics. <http://www.bluezooaquatics.com>

## Chapter Four: Purchasing Sea Monkeys

**b.) Buying in the U.K.**

Options for purchasing Sea Monkeys in the U.K. are very similar to options in the U.S. You should be able to find brine shrimp eggs at your local pet store in the aquarium section. Another option is to buy either live brine shrimp or freeze-dried eggs online. Try some of the links below.

To buy Sea Monkey eggs try these suppliers:

Amazon.co.uk. <http://www.amazon.co.uk>

Cornish Crispa Co. <http://www.cornishcrispa.co.uk>

Fish and Fits. <http://www.fishandfits.co.uk>

You can also buy live brine shrimp online:

Aquamania. <http://www.aquamania.co.uk>

Aquatics to Your Door.
<http://www.aquaticstoyourdoor.co.uk>

Yorkshire Brine Shrimp Supplies. <http://ybssuk.com/>

---

**\*\*Note:** When purchasing animals online, you often have to worry about issues of cruelty because the animals can be exposed to rough handling and extreme weather during

## Chapter Four: Purchasing Sea Monkeys

shipping. Sea Monkeys are most often sold as eggs, however, or are generally protected by a shell so they are unlikely to be damaged during the shipping process.

## Chapter Four: Purchasing Sea Monkeys

## 2.) Buying Live vs. Raising from Eggs

When it comes to buying brine shrimp you have two main options to consider: live or eggs. Encapsulated eggs are certainly easier to come buy – you can often find them at your local pet store or at any number of online aquarium suppliers. Live brine shrimp, on the other hand, are not quite so common. You may be able to find them or special order them from your local pet store, but you will likely have to order them online from a large supplier.

Before you decide how you want to buy your brine shrimp, consider the pros and cons of each option:

**Buying Live Brine Shrimp**

Pros:
- No need for hatchery equipment, already hatched
- Can transfer them directly to the prepared aquarium
- Good option if you don't want to wait
- May already be used to accepting certain foods

Cons:
- May not know how old they are (lifespan is only 1-2 years on average)
- Somewhat more expensive than purchasing eggs
- May have some difficulty in acclimating to a new tank

## Chapter Four: Purchasing Sea Monkeys

- Might be exposed to rough handling/extreme temperatures during shipping process

**Raising Brine Shrimp from Eggs**

Pros:
- Very inexpensive to purchase
- Easy to find – available in pet stores and online
- Don't have to worry about damage during shipping
- An exciting and educational process

Cons:
- Takes extra time to hatch from eggs
- May require special hatchery equipment for eggs e.g. hydrometer, air pump etc
- Eggs are not guaranteed to hatch

# Chapter Five: Caring for Sea Monkeys

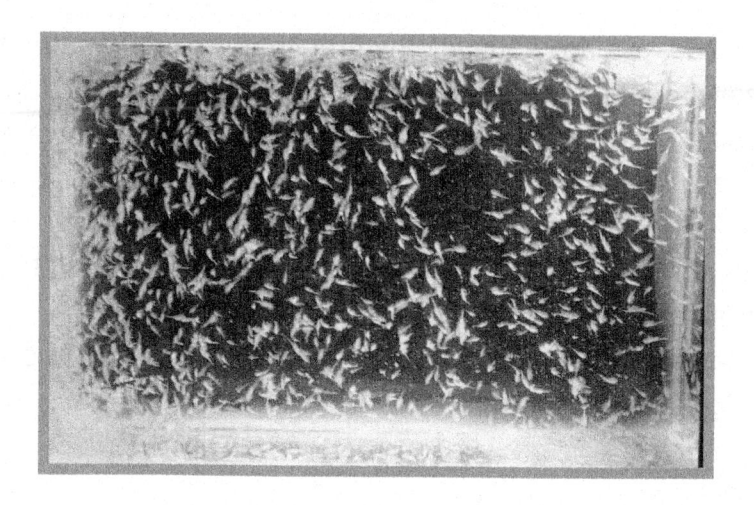

The key to keeping your Sea Monkeys happy and healthy is to provide them with an adequate diet and good habitat. In this chapter you will learn the basics about the nutritional needs of brine shrimp so you can provide them with a healthy diet.

You will also learn about their habitat requirements so you can create and stock your tank properly. With this information, you should have no problem raising your Sea Monkeys from eggs and having them lead a long and healthy life.

## Chapter Five: Caring for Sea Monkeys

## 1.) Where Do They Live?

Sea Monkeys are aquatic creatures that are found naturally in saltwater lakes all over the world. They can also be found in salt swamps near the coast and in other bodies of water with any salt content. What makes these creatures unique is their ability to adapt to a variety of conditions including various salinity levels. While seawater contains about 3.5% salt, some Sea Monkey habitats have 50% salt concentration. In their natural habitats they can also tolerate a range of temperatures.

### a.) Choosing a Tank

The ideal captive habitat for Sea Monkeys is a plastic or glass tank filled with saltwater. Though brine shrimp can tolerate fresh water for small periods of time, they will die after 4 to 5 hours in fresh water. The recommended water temperature for Sea Monkeys is between 70 and 80°F (21 to 26.6°C), though hatching temperatures are at the top of this range. A pH range between 6.0 and 9.0 is acceptable, but the ideal is around 8.0.

The design of the tank is up to you, so be as creative as you like. In the next section you will read about Sea Monkey kits that often come with a colorful plastic tank, but you can easily create a tank yourself. Simply take a large plastic container or a small glass aquarium and furnish it to meet your Sea Monkey's needs. It is not necessary to line the

## Chapter Five: Caring for Sea Monkeys

bottom of the tank with substrate (like gravel or sand), but you may want to add a few decorations to spruce up your Sea Monkey tank.

### b.) Fun Decorations for Sea Monkey Tanks

When it comes to decorating your tank, you can be as creative as you like – just be sure not to overcrowd the tank or your brine shrimp won't have room to swim. Some of the best decorations for these tanks include fake plants, small rocks, shells and even novelty aquarium décor items. You should avoid using live plants in your tank because they are unlikely to survive in salt water.

Don't be afraid to use unconventional items to decorate your Sea Monkey tank – who knows, they might enjoy it! Try using colored glass stones, an old teacup or even a glass bottle. Not only will these items give your tank a unique flair, but your Sea Monkeys will have fun swimming around the decorations. You can even change the décor scheme of your tank as often as you like.

Before you add any decorations to your Sea Monkey tank, be sure to clean them carefully with warm water. You can use a little bit of soap to clean the decorations, as long as you rinse them very well afterwards to get rid of any soap residue as soap suds can be extremely harmful to most aquatic life. If you are cleaning the decorations you've already had in your Sea Monkey tank you generally do not

## Chapter Five: Caring for Sea Monkeys

need to remove the Sea Monkeys from the tank – just carefully remove the decorations wash and then rinse them thoroughly. After replacing the decorations, be sure to wash your hands.

## Chapter Five: Caring for Sea Monkeys

### c.) Tank Maintenance

Sea Monkeys do not require a significant amount of care, but you do need to maintain their tank properly to keep them healthy. These pets are typically kept in small tanks which are fine because Sea Monkeys themselves are very small. It is important to realize, however, that wastes and toxins build up more quickly in a small tank than in a large tank – because the water volume is low, these toxins may become highly concentrated which can cause a problem for your pets.

In order to keep your tank healthy you will need to perform routine water changes where you 'clean' the tank and will then need to replace around 15-25% of the water.

The amount of times you need to do this is a matter of great debate online – with some sites recommending twice a week whilst others say you should never do it!

The right thing to do is going to be dependent on the conditions in, and size of, your tank. It's normal for there to be some algae growth in your tank and the Sea Monkeys love this but if it stops smelling like fresh grass and gets too gunky and cloudy then it is worth performing a partial water change. Frequency will be condition dependent – from every month (or more if required) to twice a year if everything still looks and smells fresh.

## Chapter Five: Caring for Sea Monkeys

A partial water change simply involves siphoning out a portion of the tank water (usually 15% to 25%) and replacing it with prepared new salt water.

Please note: If you have bought a pre-packaged kit you may be advised in the instructions it came with to only ever top up with distilled or bottled water and if this is the case you are best advised to follow those instructions and then only add a bit more salt if needed once you've checked the salinity levels with your hydrometer.

To perform a tank clean, you can buy an aquarium gravel vacuum. When performing water changes, be sure to concentrate on the accumulated food and waste at the bottom of the tank. In addition to removing accumulated debris, routine water changes will also ensure that the oxygen levels in your tank water remain high.

An aquarium gravel vacuum is a simple device made of plastic tubing – you put one end in your tank and submerge the other end to create a siphon effect. The siphon effect sucks water from the Sea Monkey tank into a bucket or container where you place the other end of the tube. Using this method, you can remove dirty water from the tank without having to remove your Sea Monkeys, then replace the water with clean water. When using a gravel vacuum, position a lamp near one side of your Sea Monkey tank. This will draw the attention of your pets, causing them all to move over to that area so you don't have to worry about them getting sucked up the tube.

## Chapter Five: Caring for Sea Monkeys

Another aspect of maintaining your Sea Monkey tank is keeping the salinity within the proper range. The ideal salinity for a Sea Monkey tank is between 30 and 35 ppt, though they can tolerate a wide range. To prepare the water for your Sea Monkey tank, simply dissolve 2 tablespoons of non-iodized salt (like synthetic sea salt) in 1 liter (1/4 gallon) of dechlorinated tap water. To dechlorinate tap water, all you have to do is use a few drops of water purifier – follow the instructions on the bottle for the proper dosage.

Installing an air stone in your Sea Monkey tank will help to keep the salt from settling and will also keep the oxygen levels within the proper range for your Sea Monkeys. An air stone is simply an air pump to which a plastic tube is connected – at the end of the tube is a porous stone (porous means it has holes in it, like a sponge). As the air pump pushes air through the tube, it goes through the air stone and produces bubbles which move the water in the tank.

You'll probably find that you don't need an air stone on all the time – a couple of times a week for a few hours should be fine. Make sure that the air stone is set on low and is producing bubbles rather than a mist or spray as this could cause problems for the brine shrimp.

## Chapter Five: Caring for Sea Monkeys

### d.) Summary of Facts

**Tank Materials**: plastic or glass

**Tank Temperature**: ideally around between 70 and 80°F (21 to 26.6°C)

**Hatching Temperature**: around 80°F (26.6°C)

**pH Level**: 6.0 to 9.0; ideal 8.0

**Salinity Level**: 30 to 35 ppt

**Saltwater Preparation**: 2 tablespoons non-iodized salt per liter water (1/4 gallon), OR follow your pre-packaged Sea Monkey kit instructions

**Tank Maintenance**: 15-25% water change as needed

**Tank Décor**: fake plants, small stones, shells, novelty aquarium décor items

# Chapter Five: Caring for Sea Monkeys

## 2.) Feeding Your Sea Monkeys

In addition to providing your Sea Monkeys with a habitat in which to live, you must also give them an adequate diet. Sea Monkeys are a type of crustacean and, as many crustaceans do, they feed on algae and various phytoplankton. This being the case, you may need to purchase special food for your Sea Monkeys. If you buy a Sea Monkey kit, you will likely receive a small supply of food but, after that runs out, you should know what kind of food to buy for your pets and where to get it.

### a.) What Do They Eat?

A crustacean is a type of animal that has a hard shell (or skeleton) on the outside of its body but no bones inside. Brine shrimp are filter feeders – this means that they gather their food from the water. In the wild, brine shrimp feed on various forms of algae and phytoplankton once they reach adulthood. They eat this type of food because it is the right size for them to consume and because it is readily available in their environment.

In nauplii form (as babies), however, they feed on energy reserves that were stored in the cyst (egg) until it is depleted. This depletion normally happens around day 5 so this is when you should start feeding them and then they will need feeding again every 5 days.

## Chapter Five: Caring for Sea Monkeys

In captivity, brine shrimp can be fed powdered algae or a particulate food made of powdered algae, wheat flour, yeast and egg yolk. You should not try to collect your own phytoplankton if you live by a sea or lake because pollutants could contaminate the water – you could also accidentally introduce bacteria or other harmful substances into your tank along with the food.

### b.) How Do You Feed Them?

Feeding Sea Monkeys is a fairly simple affair because they eat their food right out of the water. So all you have to do is add the food to your Sea Monkey tank with a very small spoon. To make it easier for your Sea Monkeys to eat it, stir the food into a small amount of tank water. Using this method, the food will mix with the tank water, making it available for your Sea Monkeys at all levels in the tank.

The thing to remember when feeding your Sea Monkeys is that a little food goes a long way. Sea Monkeys are very small creatures, so each individual animal doesn't need a lot of food at any one time. You need to avoid overfeeding. Any uneaten food will simply sink to the bottom of the tank and accumulate as waste – as it breaks down, that waste will produce ammonia, a substance which can be toxic to Sea Monkeys. A good rule of thumb to follow is that, after feeding your pets, the tank water shouldn't remain cloudy for more than 15 minutes. If it stays cloudy for longer make sure you reduce the amount you feed them next time.

## Chapter Five: Caring for Sea Monkeys

Use no more than a very small pinch on the feeding spoon – it can be tempting to feed them more but this could be very harmful to their environment and hence them.

### c.) Making Sea Monkey Food at Home

While the Sea Monkey food you can get at the store is inexpensive and easy to come by, you also have the option of making Sea Monkey food at home, though it's only really recommended as an emergency measure. One way to make brine shrimp food is to create a yeast suspension. Simply take some of the water from your Sea Monkey tank, or create a salt solution of the same salinity, to start. Next, stir in enough baker's yeast to give the water a milky appearance, then refrigerate the suspension until you are ready to use it.

Another thing you can try if you've run out of regular Sea Monkey food is to boil an egg, mix a little bit of just the yolk with some water and put that into the tank for them to eat.

Again with home made food make sure you don't overfeed the Sea Monkeys - they only need a small amount to survive.

## Chapter Five: Caring for Sea Monkeys

### d.) Summary of Facts

**Feeding Type**: non-selective filter feeder
**Diet in Wild**: algae and phytoplankton
**Captive Diet**: powdered algae, wheat flour, yeast, egg yolk
**Feeding Frequency**: for hatchlings not until day 5, for adults once every 5 days
**Feeding Amount**: small pinch of powder
**Feeding Tips**: do not overfeed; water shouldn't remain cloudy for more than 15 minutes after feeding

# Chapter Six: Hatching and Breeding Sea Monkeys

One of the most popular methods of raising brine shrimp is to hatch them from eggs. In addition to hatching your own brine shrimp, you can also breed your own pets at home.

Female brine shrimp are capable of ovulating every 140 hours (5 to 6 days) and the eggs often hatch within a few hours of being laid which helps make them very easy to breed. In this chapter you will learn the basics about hatching Sea Monkeys from eggs and breeding your own Sea Monkeys.

## Chapter Six: Breeding Sea Monkeys

### 1.) Hatching Sea Monkeys from Eggs

Hatching Sea Monkeys from eggs is very easy to do – the first part of the method (the water preparation) that you follow is dependent on if you have purchased a pre-packaged kit or a package of eggs separately. The basic difference is that if you've purchased a kit you will need to use distilled or bottled water treated with the water purifier packet it comes with to hatch your Sea Monkeys, instead of creating a saline solution with salt.

If you have purchased an all inclusive Sea Monkey kit please make sure you follow those instructions and only use this guide to give you additional helpful information. As there are so many different kits on the market your specific instructions could be different and are of course going to contain the right information for the specific Sea Monkeys you've purchased.

**Water preparation for hatching from brine shrimp eggs:**

You just need the eggs themselves and a few other items. Some of the items you will need include:

- Spring water or tap water
- Water purifier (dechlorinating solution)
- Non-iodized salt (like synthetic sea salt)
- Brine shrimp eggs

## Chapter Six: Breeding Sea Monkeys

- Air stone and air pump
- Plastic container
- Lamp

Fill your tank with water then treat it according to the dosing instructions with a water purifier or dechlorinating solution. This solution will remove any chemicals from the tap water that could be dangerous for your pets.

Next, dissolve about 2 tablespoons of non-iodized salt like synthetic sea salt, in the water for each liter used (1/4 gallon). Check the salinity levels are 30-35ppt with your hydrometer.

**Water preparation for all-inclusive kits:**

Fill your tank with water and then treat it according to the instructions that come with your kit. In most cases this will include using the water purifying packet that comes with the kit, in filtered or bottled water, to help create a saline solution for the eggs. Once you have done this you should wait at least 24 hours for the 'purification' of the water to take effect.

**Hatching the eggs**

Drop an air stone into the tank and turn the pump up to medium-low or medium speed so it releases a steady stream of bubbles but not a fine mist. This is important as if

## Chapter Six: Breeding Sea Monkeys

the bubbles are too small the hatchlings could stick to them and die. Position a lamp near the tank to keep the water warm and to aid in the hatching.

All that is left to do is to stir in the eggs. One liter of water (1/4 gallon) is adequate for between ¼ tablespoon and 1 tablespoon of eggs (again follow any all inclusive pack instructions!). Stir the eggs into the water and ensure that the air stone keeps the eggs from sinking to the bottom of the tank. In water temperatures around 80°F (26.6°C), the eggs should hatch within 24 hours. At temperatures below this range, the eggs may take longer to hatch but be sure not to exceed temperatures of 80°F (26.6°C). Sometimes the eggs can take longer to hatch so be patient.

Once the eggs hatch, you will see clouds of baby brine shrimp swimming around – these will be tiny - about the size of a period/full stop! You may also notice a dusting of debris that sinks to the bottom – these are the unhatched eggs. The discarded shells of the hatchlings will likely float to the surface of the water so you can skim them off and discard them. After the eggs hatch, turn down the speed on the air stone and move the lamp so the light hits the center of the tank.

Sea Monkey eggs typically hatch within 24-48 hours of being exposed to saltwater. The newly hatched brine shrimp are referred to as nauplii, and they are technically the larval stage of the brine shrimp.

## Chapter Six: Breeding Sea Monkeys

In the first 5 days of their lives the brine shrimp will not need to be fed so make sure that you take note, as near as you are able to, of what day they were born on.

Don't clean your tank whilst your brine shrimp are very young as they will be more susceptible to getting sucked up in the vacuum, and to any changes in the salinity levels.

## Chapter Six: Breeding Sea Monkeys

## 2.) Breeding Sea Monkeys

Sea Monkeys are unique in that they can mate in several different ways – females can even produce eggs without the help of a male. It typically takes 6 to 8 weeks for brine shrimp to reach their adult size at which point they are ready to mate. Telling male Sea Monkeys apart from females can be tricky, but if you have a magnifying glass you should be able to manage it.

There are several differences between male and female brine shrimp, the most notable perhaps being that whilst both males and females have two sets of antenna, the males have a bigger claw-like second set, whereas the females second set is smaller. The male uses these claw-like antenna to grip the females during the mating process.

Female brine shrimp tend to be slightly longer or bigger than the males and the other thing you may be able to see by using a magnifying glass is the egg sack around the middle section of the females. If there are no eggs in the sack these will appear to be whitish but if there are eggs in them the color might be darker and you may even be able to see some of the individual eggs as well.

When male and female Sea Monkeys mate, the male will often attach to the female and cling to her for a period of several minutes to several hours while fertilizing the eggs. If there is no male present, the female can still produce fertile eggs through a process called parthenogenesis.

## Chapter Six: Breeding Sea Monkeys

Parthenogenesis is a form of reproduction which is commonly seen in plants and several invertebrates, as well as some vertebrate species. Invertebrates are animals which do not have a skeleton – some examples of invertebrates include insects, worms, nails, octopus and crabs.

When animals produce babies, typically half of the genetic material for the babies comes from the mother and half from the father. In the case of parthenogenesis, however, there is no father present so all of the genetic material (DNA) comes from the mother. The result is similar to a clone (an identical replica) of the mother. Some other animals that use this type of reproduction include some fish, amphibians, reptiles and certain types of birds.

As long as you raise your brine shrimp in the right conditions, they should be able to reproduce with or without the presence of a male.

A female brine shrimp will carry her eggs for between 5 and 20 days, though they are capable of producing eggs every 140 hours (5 to 6 days). Once released, the eggs will likely sink to the bottom of the tank where many of them will lay dormant. Some of the eggs, on the other hand, will hatch almost immediately.

Ensure that you keep your tank within the suggested temperature range as if the tank is too cold your Sea

## Chapter Six: Breeding Sea Monkeys

Monkeys will not hatch or grow. An aquarium thermometer is a really crucial bit of kit for ensuring success with breeding brine shrimp.

# Chapter Seven: Keeping Sea Monkeys Healthy

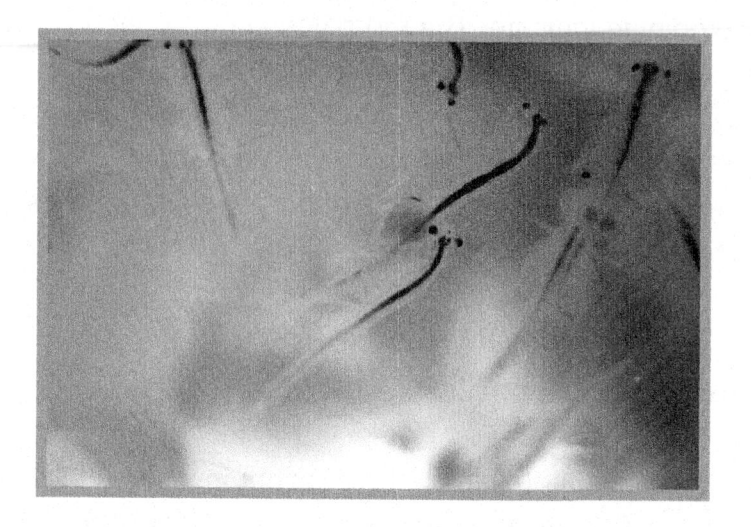

After putting in the time and effort to hatch and raise your Sea Monkeys, the last thing you want is for them to get sick. Keeping your Sea Monkeys healthy is not difficult, but there are a few things you need to know. Water quality, for example, is a key element in maintaining the health of your Sea Monkeys. In this chapter you will learn the basics about how Sea Monkeys get sick and what you can do to help them if they do.

## Chapter Seven: Keeping Sea Monkeys Healthy

### 1.) Do Brine Shrimp Get Sick?

Like any animal, brine shrimp are prone to getting sick at some point in their life. The more you know about possible illnesses, the better equipped you will be to handle them when they occur. If you want your Sea Monkeys to stand the best chance of survival and recovery, familiarize yourself with common diseases and treatments such as those covered in this chapter.

### a.) Common Brine Shrimp Illnesses

The key to ensuring that your brine shrimp make a full recovery is to take decisive action as soon as possible. The sooner you identify the problem, the sooner you can get your pets the right treatment and set them on the road to recovery. Unfortunately, it can be difficult to diagnose diseases because these animals are so small. On the other hand, the treatment for many diseases is the same, so you have a little room for error.

In this section you will learn the basics about some of the most common health problems affecting brine shrimp. Some of the illnesses or conditions you may encounter include:

- Cestode Parasites
- Leucothrix Bacteria
- Not Hatching

# Chapter Seven: Keeping Sea Monkeys Healthy

- Overcrowding
- Starvation
- Stress
- Vibrio sp. Bacteria

## Cestode Parasites

A parasite is a type of organism that attaches to another organism (a host body) and feeds from it in order to grow. Cestode parasites, or tapeworm parasites, are fairly common in the natural environment where brine shrimp live – particularly in the Great Salt Lake. These parasites may be introduced into the environment by migratory birds that visit the lake through their excrement. The brine shrimp are exposed to the parasite through contaminated water and then become hosts for the parasites.

In reality, brine shrimp serve as an intermediate host for the tapeworm parasites. They provide a host in which the tapeworm can develop and, when the brine shrimp are eaten, the mature tapeworm is passed on to another animal. Brine shrimp that are infected with the tapeworm parasite may be dark red in color.

One option in treating brine shrimp diseases like parasites is to increase the salinity in the tank. Be careful not to increase the salinity in the tank too much or it could have a detrimental effect on your Sea Monkeys. Start by adding a ¼ teaspoon of extra salt, mixing it with some tank water before adding it to the tank. Slowly increase the salt concentration over 2 to 3 days, adding ¼ teaspoon extra salt every 6 to 8 hours. This should help to kill any bacteria or parasites in the tank. After the treatment is completed, perform a water change to bring the salinity level back to normal.

## Leucothrix Bacteria

Bacteria are present in all bodies of water and on many other surfaces and it is not always harmful. One kind of bacteria that can be harmful to brine shrimp, however, is called Leucothrix mucor. This type of bacteria is fairly common in Sea Monkey tanks and it can be deadly, killing them if not properly controlled. The infection does not become fatal immediately though – it happens over time. The bacteria first attach to the gills of the Sea Monkeys, eventually moving on to the swimming appendages, antennae and other surfaces.

Because this type of bacteria is filamentous, it forms a sort of mesh around the body of the brine shrimp. This mesh traps and holds a variety of microorganisms and various types of debris which may also damage the Sea Monkey. Various treatments have been tested against these bacteria including antibiotic medications like formalin, potassium permanganate, terramycin and cutrine.

# Chapter Seven: Keeping Sea Monkeys Healthy

You can often find these medications in the aquarium aisle at your local pet store – if you can't find them there or online you may also be able to get them from a veterinarian. To use these treatments, you will need to dose the water in your tank according to the size of your tank – follow the dosing instructions on the package carefully to find the right amount for your particular tank. To dose the tank, all you need to do is stir the right amount of medication right into the tank water – you can also stir it into a cup of tank water then pour that into the tank.

## Not Hatching

Not all of your brine shrimp eggs are going to hatch the first time around. The fact of the matter is that some are simply slow hatchers. If you find that a significant number of your eggs fail to hatch, remove them from the tank and place them in a new tank of saltwater. In most cases, the eggs hatch the second time around. It is also possible that the thickness of the protective shells around the cysts causes them to take longer to hatch. Don't panic right away – give the eggs some extra time and then try for a second time.

## Overcrowding

Overcrowding occurs when you keep too many Sea Monkeys in the tank. This could occur if your tank is too small or if you simply hatch more Sea Monkeys than your tank can handle. The number of Sea Monkeys that hatch from your eggs may vary, so do not try to hatch too many at once. Sea Monkeys only require about $1/10^{th}$ of an ounce of water each so you can easily keep 100 Sea Monkeys in a tank that holds about 12 ounces of water.

If the tank becomes overcrowded, your Sea Monkeys could become stressed and may be more susceptible to disease. Overcrowding can also result in a faster accumulation of detritus and debris which will have a negative impact on the water quality in your Sea Monkey tank – this, too, could negatively affect the health of your pets.

**Starvation**

In brine shrimp, starvation can occur due to a number of factors. The most obvious, of course, is inadequate feeding. If you do not offer your Sea Monkeys the right type of food or underfeed them, they will not develop properly and could actually end up starving. Some foods you should not feed your Sea Monkeys include aquarium fish food, vegetables, bread or other human food.

If you can regularly see a thin black line along the backs of some of your pets then this should give you some comfort that they are not starving. This black line is their digestive system and if it is black then this is indicative of it being full.

# Chapter Seven: Keeping Sea Monkeys Healthy

Another surprising factor which may contribute to the starvation of your Sea Monkeys is the aeration of your tank. If you use a wooden air stone or some other type of air stone that produces a really fine mist of bubbles in the tank water, it could clog the feeding system of your Sea Monkeys, causing them to starve. Aeration is important for the health of your Sea Monkeys, but you need to be careful not to let the air bubbles get too fine – the bubbles are too fine if you cannot distinguish individual bubbles and if they are not separated from each other.

Some keepers of brine shrimp prefer not to have an air stone and oxygenate their tanks by blowing into their tanks with a clean straw for a few minutes a day. An issue with this method is that your breath also contains carbon dioxide so it's not a foolproof method. If you don't have an air stone you can stir your tank with a plastic spoon for a few minutes each day which should help to oxygenate the water.

## Stress

Stress is not a disease, but it plays a significant role in the health of your Sea Monkeys. When sudden changes occur in the tank – such as tank temperature or salinity levels – it can have a drastic effect on your pets stress levels. Their bodies may no longer function in the way they are meant to and they could then become stressed. As their stress level increases, your Sea Monkeys' immune systems will suffer

## Chapter Seven: Keeping Sea Monkeys Healthy

and they will become more susceptible to contracting any of the diseases discussed in this section.

### Vibrio sp. Bacteria

Vibrio is a genus of bacteria that is commonly found in aquatic saltwater environments. This type of bacteria is gram-negative and, under a microscope, is seen to have a curved rod shape. Vibrio sp. Bacteria is particularly likely to be seen in brine shrimp tanks due to the protein-richness of the water – this is often due to accumulated waste and uneaten food at the bottom of the tank.

In the case of bacterial infections, you should treat your tank with some kind of antibiotic medication. The most popular types are formalin, potassium permanganate and terramycin. You should be able to find these medications in the aquarium aisle at your local pet store. Be sure to follow the dosing instructions closely to avoid overdosing your Sea Monkeys. In addition to dosing the tank with medication, you may also need to perform routine partial water changes throughout the course of treatment.

### 2.) Keeping Sea Monkeys Healthy

The best method of treating Sea Monkey diseases is, unsurprisingly, to prevent them from happening in the first place. While it is fairly easy to prevent your Sea Monkeys from getting sick, it does require a certain degree of effort.

# Chapter Seven: Keeping Sea Monkeys Healthy

In this section you will learn about some of the key elements of preventing your pets from getting sick.

## Maintaining High Water Quality

For your Sea Monkeys, their tank is their home so if the water is really unclean, they aren't going to be healthy. There are a number of factors that play into the water quality in your Sea Monkey tank. Another name for water quality is "water chemistry" because it is largely influenced by certain chemistry levels in the tank water – water hardness, pH, ammonia levels, and more.

Some aspects of water quality and water chemistry are more applicable to home aquariums than Sea Monkey tanks, but the same general rules apply. In order to maintain high water quality in your tank, you will need to perform periodic water changes – depending on conditions in your tank. You should also ensure that your tank is properly aerated with an air pump and/or an aquarium filter.

To make sure the chemistry levels in your Sea Monkey tank are within the proper limits, you may want to consider testing your tank water once a week. Many pet stores will test aquarium water for free – you can also buy a test kit and perform the test yourself at home. In most cases, all you have to do is dip a paper strip into a sample of tank water and compare the color of the strip to a color chart that comes with the kit. If any of your tank's chemistry levels are out of line, you will be able to make changes before it affects the health of your Sea Monkeys.

## Establishing the Nitrogen Cycle

The nitrogen cycle is the process through which a colony of beneficial bacteria becomes established in an aquarium, working to convert the ammonia and nitrite produced by the breakdown of wastes into less-harmful substances like nitrate. When it comes to bacteria, you may think that all of it is harmful, having the potential to cause disease. In reality, however, bacteria play an essential role in the health of an aquarium.

It takes time for the nitrogen cycle to become established in any new tank. It is particularly important in large aquariums, but it can also play a big role in smaller Sea Monkey tanks. Not only does it help to ensure the proper breakdown of waste, but the nitrogen cycle also helps to remove that dissolved waste from the tank water – this is essential in tanks with a smaller water volume.

In general, all you have to do for the nitrogen cycle to become established in your tank is to wait – it normally takes in the region of 4 to 6 weeks for the nitrogen cycle to establish itself. As your Sea Monkeys eat food and produce waste, these products will become food for beneficial bacteria and they will naturally begin to colonize your tank. Over time, the bacteria will establish a colony that is the

## Chapter Seven: Keeping Sea Monkeys Healthy

right size for your tank so you do not have to worry about making any adjustments – the bacteria will reproduce as the number of Sea Monkeys in your tank grows.

Keeping the tank clean through partial water changes can be helpful in maintaining a healthy nitrogen balance. If you don't do a partial change when the water smells off and is very cloudy a long time after you have fed your brine shrimp, the levels of the ammonia could rise to levels which can be harmful to your pets. To prevent your Sea Monkeys getting sick you therefore need to make sure that you do change 15-25% of the water when the tank gets unclean.

**Oxygenating the Water**

Oxygen levels in your Sea Monkey tank are incredibly important. Not only do high oxygen levels help to maintain good water quality, they also affect the development of your Sea Monkeys. With high oxygen levels, brine shrimp can develop from hatchlings into adult in as few as 8 days. If oxygen levels are low, however, they could fail to develop properly and may even die.

There is no way to test the oxygen levels in your Sea Monkey tank without investing in some expensive equipment. There is no reason you need that equipment, however, if you keep your tank clean. As your Sea Monkeys breathe, they take oxygen from the tank water and their bodies convert it into carbon dioxide as it is exhaled. Thus,

# Chapter Seven: Keeping Sea Monkeys Healthy

the oxygen levels in your water tank go down over time. The best way to handle this is to have an oxygenating system like an air stone or pump and also to perform routine partial water changes when needed so the water in your tank is always fresh and full of oxygen for your pets.

## Proper Temperature and Salinity

While Sea Monkeys are naturally found in waters of various temperature, each species has adapted to a certain environment. It is also important to note that brine shrimp are ectothermic animals – they are incapable of regulating their own body temperature so they rely on the temperature of their environment. Essential bodily functions like digestion and respiration work best within a certain temperature range and, for Sea Monkeys, that range is between 70 and 80°F (21 to 26.6°C), in most cases.

Not only can the bodily functions of your Sea Monkeys be affected by tank temperatures that are too high or too low, but an imbalance either way could also cause them to become stressed. Like all animals, when sea monkeys are stressed they are more prone to develop illnesses. For this reason, it is essential that you maintain the proper temperature and salinity levels in your Sea Monkey tank.

Maintaining the salinity and temperature in your tank may require you to test your tank water on a regular basis, but it is definitely worth the extra effort. To test the temperature,

# Chapter Seven: Keeping Sea Monkeys Healthy

all you need is an aquarium thermometer. To increase the tank temperature, use an aquarium heater or a lamp placed by the tank to slowly warm the water. If the temperature is too high, do not be tempted to add cold water to the tank – simply remove the lamp or aquarium heater and let the water cool naturally. To change the salinity in your tank, perform a partial water change – to increase the salinity, add extra salt to the water and, to decrease it, use less salt than usual during this change.

# Chapter Eight: Sea Monkeys Care Sheet

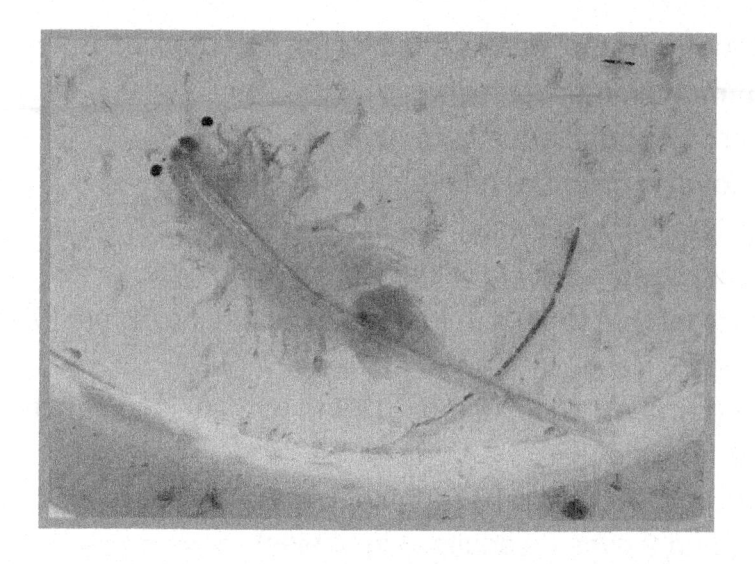

This book is full of information regarding the care and keeping of Sea Monkeys. There may come a time, however, when you need a quick answer to a question and don't want to flip through the book to find it – that is where this chapter comes in. In this chapter you will find a quick-reference guide for all the basics on brine shrimp including general information, a habitat set-up guide, nutritional information and breeding tips. Before you go elsewhere for information, check this chapter.

# Chapter Eight: Sea Monkeys Care Sheet

## 1.) Basic Information

**Scientific Name**: genus Artemia, family Artemiidae
**Common Name**: brine shrimp
**Type of Animal**: aquatic crustacean
**Discovery**: historical records date back to 982
**Habitat:** inland saltwater lakes, worldwide
**Adaptations:** ability to withstand salinity of 25% to 250%
**Size (male):** 8 to 10 mm (0.31 to 0.39 in) long, 4 mm (0.16 in) wide
**Size (female):** 10 to 12 mm (0.39 to 0.47 in) long, 4 mm (0.16 in) wide
**Anatomy**: body has 19 segments; three sections including a tail and 2 eyes (in adults, 3 in babies)
**Reproduction**: eggs; can lay dormant for years
**Ovulation**: every 140 hours
**Eggs**: may hatch immediately after laying; can lay dormant for up to 10 years in anaerobic conditions
**Common Use**: live food for fish and crustaceans, aquatic pets, biological research, etc.

# Chapter Eight: Sea Monkeys Care Sheet

## 2.) Habitat Set-Up Guide

**Tank Materials**: plastic or glass
**Tank Temperature**: ideally around between 70 and 80°F (21 to 26.6°C)
**Hatching Temperature**: 80°F (26.6°C)
**pH Level**: 6.0 to 9.0; ideal 8.0
**Salinity Level**: 30 to 35 ppt
**Saltwater Preparation**: 2 tablespoons non-iodized salt per liter water (1/4 gallon) or follow your pre-packaged kit instructions
**Tank Maintenance**: 15-25% water change periodically
**Tank Décor**: fake plants, small stones, shells, novelty aquarium décor items

## 3.) Nutritional Information

**Feeding Type**: non-selective filter feeder
**Diet in Wild**: algae and phytoplankton
**Captive Diet**: powdered algae, wheat flour, yeast, egg yolk
**Feeding Frequency**: when first hatched after 5 days, after that every 5 days
**Feeding Amount**: small pinch of powder
**Feeding Tips**: do not overfeed; water should not remain cloudy for more than 15 minutes after feeding

## 4.) Hatching

**Tank Type**: plastic or glass tank
**Salt Concentration**: 2 tablespoons salt per liter (1/4 gallon) water OR follow your pre-packaged Sea Monkey kit instructions
**Other Equipment**: air stone, air pump, lamp
**Hatching Temperature**: around 80°F (26.6°C)
**Hatching Time**: within 24-48 hours average
**Reproduction Methods**: mating or parthenogenesis
**Mating Length**: several minutes to several hours
**Gestation Period**: 5 to 20 days
**After Hatching**: skim off discarded shells, turn down air stone speed

# Chapter Nine: Common Mistakes Owners Make

If you have never owned brine shrimp before, you probably have a few questions. Luckily, these pets are fairly easy to keep and they don't require a great deal of care or extra equipment. As you learn how to care for them, however, you are likely to make a few mistakes along the way. To minimize any consequences for your Sea Monkeys during this trial period, you should learn about some of the most common mistakes brine shrimp owners make. By informing yourself about these mistakes, you can avoid making them yourself.

# Chapter Nine: Common Mistakes Owners Make

## 1.) Inadequate Aeration

When it comes to hatching Sea Monkey eggs, aeration is extremely important. Decapsulated eggs (cysts which have had their protective shell removed) will have lost their natural buoyancy, so aeration of the tank water is essential for keeping the eggs afloat. If you do not properly aerate the tank during hatching, your brine shrimp eggs will all sink to the bottom of the tank and collect there. As a result, only a small number of the eggs will actually hatch.

Aeration in the Sea Monkey tank is also important as a means of oxygenating the tank water. All animals require oxygen for respiration and your brine shrimp draw their oxygen from the tank water. Installing a small air stone in your tank is the best way to aerate your tank water, but be sure to only have it on low or your Sea Monkeys could have trouble swimming. You may find you only need to use the air stone a couple a times a week – you will know if the aeration in your tank gets too low if your Sea Monkeys begin crowding around the surface of the tank water. Sometimes Sea Monkeys will turn pink when they don't have enough oxygen in the tank so this is also something to watch out for.

If you do not have an air stone or pump it is possible to oxygenate the water by stirring a plastic spoon around in the water for 3-5 minutes a day to help move some oxygen through the water. Some people recommend blowing through a straw into the water but you can end up blowing

## Chapter Nine: Common Mistakes Owners Make

carbon dioxide from your lungs so it's probably best to use this method only in emergencies!

Chapter Nine: Common Mistakes Owners Make

## 2.) Overcrowding/Small Tank

Brine shrimp do need some space in order to thrive and grow. If you have ever experienced claustrophobia, or have simply had to spend time in a cramped space, imagine living your entire life that way. Doesn't sound very comfortable, does it? Without adequate space, your brine shrimp may not grow properly and they could also become stressed.

Overcrowding can occur in two situations. First, your brine shrimp tank is too small. While many Sea Monkey tanks that come with all-inclusive kits are small, that doesn't mean small is the only option for them. Another possibility is that you simply have too many brine shrimp in the tank. If the tank becomes overcrowded not only can your Sea Monkeys become stressed, but it could also lead to a quicker accumulation of debris and waste which could decrease the water quality in your tank.

If it looks like your Sea Monkeys barely have any room to move – if they seem to be swimming on top of each other – they are probably overcrowded. If your Sea Monkeys begin to suddenly die off, it could also be a sign of overcrowding. You can try hatching your eggs in small batches so you don't end up with too many at once.

## Chapter Nine: Common Mistakes Owners Make

### 3.) Fluctuating Water Parameters

While brine shrimp can adapt to a variety of different conditions, they do best when those conditions remain stable. It is true that brine shrimp can survive in salinity concentrations of 50% or more, but that doesn't mean they do well in varying concentrations. The specific salinity of your Sea Monkey tank is not nearly as important as keeping that salinity stable – most owners recommend dissolving 2 tablespoons of salt in 1 liter (1/4 gallon) of water. If you keep up this concentration, your pets should be just fine.

If you want to check the salinity in your tank, you can invest in a device called a hydrometer or simply take a sample of tank water to your local pet store for free testing. It is a good idea to check your tank salinity on a weekly basis, if not more often, to prevent problems. If you do need to change the salinity quickly, you can do so with a significant water change – just increase or decrease the amount of salt you normally use when preparing the water for your water change.

Another water parameter you have to worry about is the temperature of your tank. Sea Monkeys are ectothermic creatures which means that they rely on the temperature of their environment to regulate their body temperature. Sea Monkeys thrive best in a temperature range between 70 and 80°F (21 to 26.6°C). Unless the temperature in your home remains steady, you may want to use a lamp or

## Chapter Nine: Common Mistakes Owners Make

aquarium heater to ensure that your Sea Monkey tank stays within the proper water temperature range.

# Chapter Ten: Frequently Asked Questions

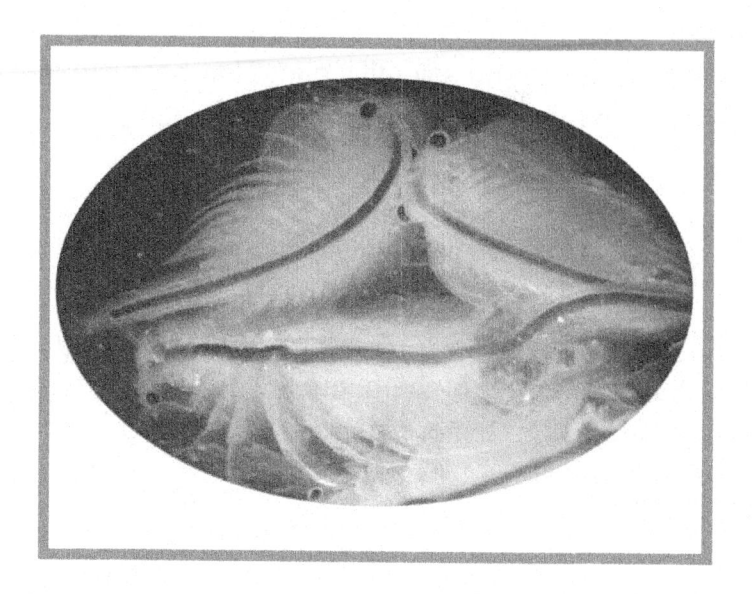

After reading this book, you may feel like an expert on Sea Monkeys – and perhaps you are! You may, however, still find yourself with a few questions. Don't worry, that is completely normal. In this chapter you will find a selection of some of the most frequently asked questions about Sea Monkeys and brine shrimp so you can bolster your already significant store of knowledge. In this chapter you will find the answers to questions regarding care, housing, breeding, feeding and more.

## Chapter Ten: Frequently Asked Questions

**Q**: What are Sea Monkeys?

**A**: In short, Sea Monkeys are actually a type of brine shrimp, a type of aquatic crustacean that lives in saltwater lakes and swamps. The scientific name for these creatures is Artemia and there are several different species.

**Q**: How long do Sea Monkeys live?

**A**: The lifespan of your Sea Monkeys depends largely on how well you take care of them, but the average lifespan is about 1-2 years. The better you care for your Sea Monkeys, the longer they will live.

**Q**: Why did my Sea Monkeys die all of a sudden?

**A**: There are several potential causes for the sudden death of your brine shrimp. The tank could be overcrowded or you might have overfed your pets, causing waste and toxins to build up to high levels. If the temperature in your tank gets too hot or cold, that could also kill off your Sea Monkeys within a short period of time.

**Q**: Why can't I use tap water in my Sea Monkey tank?

**A**: You can use tap water in your tank as long as you treat it with a water purifier first. Tap water is treated with a number

## Chapter Ten: Frequently Asked Questions

of chemicals like chlorine which make it safe for human to drink but can be dangerous for aquatic animals like Sea Monkeys. Treating tap water with water purifiers such as dechlorinating solutions makes it safe for brine shrimp to live in. Alternatively use bottled filtered or distilled water, especially if you have purchased a kit which instructs you to do so.

**Q**: Will all of my Sea Monkey eggs hatch?

**A**: The number of eggs that hatch out of any bunch varies. It is unlikely that all of your eggs will hatch, but even those that don't can be gathered up and put in a new saltwater solution for a second try.

**Q**: What affects the hatching rate of brine shrimp?

**A**: The number of eggs that hatch and the period of time it takes them to hatch may vary according to a number of different factors. Aeration is incredibly important, as is a proper light source and adequate water salinity and temperature. If all of these conditions are correct, your brine shrimp eggs should hatch within 24-48 hours.

**Q**: Should I start feeding my Sea Monkeys immediately?

## Chapter Ten: Frequently Asked Questions

**A**: No, for a few days after they hatch your Sea Monkeys will subsist on stored energy from their eggs. You should wait until 5 days after they hatch to start feeding them.

**Q**: Can I just sprinkle the food in my Sea Monkey tank?

**A**: You can sprinkle the food directly onto your tank water, but a better method of feeding your Sea Monkeys is to mix the food with a little tank water. This ensures that the food is evenly distributed throughout the tank. Remember a tiny pinch goes a long way!

**Q**: Do I need a filter for my Sea Monkey tank?

**A**: You shouldn't need a filter unless you have a very large tank or a significantly large number of Sea Monkeys. You should, however, ideally install an air pump in your tank to keep the water aerated and oxygenated for your pets. Aeration is especially important when you are trying to hatch your Sea Monkey eggs.

**Q**: Why are my Sea Monkeys gathered at the surface?

**A**: When your Sea Monkeys all gather near the top of the tank, it is often an indication that the oxygen levels in your tank water are too low (they may also turn pinkish in color). To remedy this problem, install an air pump or turn up the

## Chapter Ten: Frequently Asked Questions

speed a little on your air stone (not so high that you can't see individual bubbles or the Sea Monkeys seem to have trouble swimming).

**Q:** Why are there particles floating around the tank?

**A:** If your Sea Monkeys have just hatched, the particles floating around in the tank might be their discarded shells. It is also possible that particles of uneaten food are floating around in the tank. You can skim off these particles with a net but if it does look like food then this is a pretty good sign you are overfeeding your pets.

**Q:** At what temperature should I keep my tank?

**A:** The ideal water temperature range for Sea Monkeys is between 70 and 80°F (21 to 26.6°C). You can choose any temperature within this range, as long as you keep it stable. If the temperature falls below 60°F (15.5°C) or above 80°F (26.6°C) the Sea Monkeys may fall ill and even die so do watch the temperature.

It is worth investing in an aquarium thermometer as they don't cost much and are extremely useful. If the water is too cold try positioning the tank in indirect sunlight or use a lamp to heat the water gently.

## Chapter Ten: Frequently Asked Questions

**Q**: Do I have to clean my Sea Monkey tank?

**A**: You do not need to "clean" the tank in the traditional sense, meaning that you shouldn't have to scrub the walls or anything like that. You do need to change about 15-25% of the tank volume when the water gets really unclean or smells rotten to keep the water quality in the tank high.

# Chapter Eleven: Relevant Websites

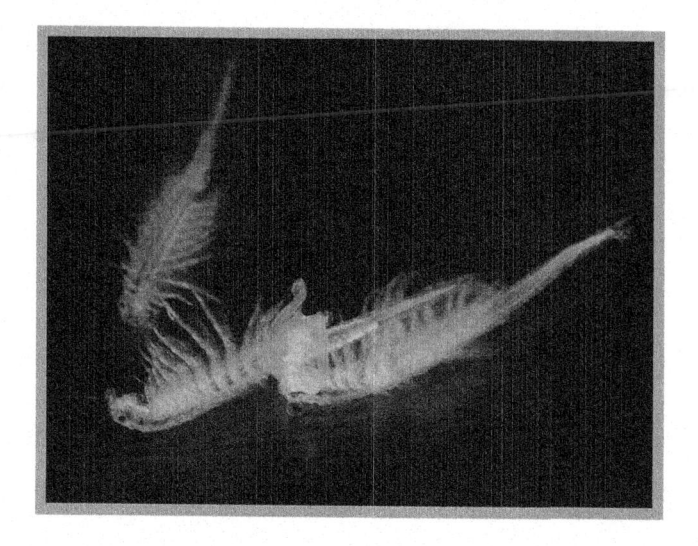

After reading this book you should have a better understanding of what Sea Monkeys are and how to care for them. There may come a time, however, when you need some more information and require additional resources. In this chapter you will find a list of relevant websites for information on Sea Monkey-related topics including:

        Food for Sea Monkeys
        Aquariums for Sea Monkeys
        Health Info for Sea Monkeys
        General Info on Sea Monkeys

Chapter Eleven: Relevant Websites

## 1.) Food for Sea Monkeys

In this section you will find a number of resources regarding food for Sea Monkeys including websites to buy food as well as general information about feeding.

**United States Websites**:

"O.S.I. Artemia Food." Drs. Foster and Smith. <http://www.drsfostersmith.com/ >

"Artemia (Brine Shrimp) FAQ 1.1." The Computer Action Team. <http://web.cecs.pdx.edu/>

Emslie, Sara. "Artemia salina." Animal Diversity Web: University of Michigan Museum of Zoology. <http://animaldiversity.ummz.umich.edu/>

# Chapter Eleven: Relevant Websites

**United Kingdom Websites**:

"Food and Feeding Sea Monkeys." SeaMonkey-Shop.co.uk.
<http://www.seamonkey-shop.co.uk>

"Dan's Artemia Feed with Beta Glucan." ZM Fish Food.
<http://www.zmsystems.co.uk/>

"Brine Shrimp Feed." ReefPhyto.co.uk.
<http://www.reefphyto.co.uk/all-products/brine-shrimp-feed.html>

"Brine Shrimp Food 25ml." Aquarium Supplies UK.
<http://aquarium-suppliesuk.co.uk/Brine-Shrimp-Food-25ml>

NT Labs.
<http://www.ntlabs.co.uk/>

## Chapter Eleven: Relevant Websites

## 2.) Aquariums for Sea Monkeys

In this section you will find a number of resources regarding hatcheries for Sea Monkeys including websites to buy aquariums and tanks.

**United States Websites:**

"Brine Shrimp Aquarium." Drs. Foster and Smith.
<http://www.drsfostersmith.com/>

Marine Depot USA
<http://www.marinedepot.com>

Pet Smart USA. <http://www.petsmart.com>

## Chapter Eleven: Relevant Websites

**United Kingdom Websites**:

Amazon.com.
<http://www.amazon.co.uk/>

Pets at Home
<http://www.petsathome.com>

Swell UK
<http://www.swelluk.com>

## 3.) Health Info for Sea Monkeys

In this section you will find a number of resources regarding the health of Sea Monkeys.

**United States Websites:**

Marques, Antonia., et al. "Effects of Bacteria on Artemia franciscana Cultured in Different Gnotobiotic Environments." Applied and Environmental Microbiology. 2005 August; 71(8): 4307-4317.
<http://www.ncbi.nlm.nih.gov/>

"Brine Shrimp 2: Brine Shrimp Survival." AAAS Science NetLinks. <http://sciencenetlinks.com/>

"Brine Shrimp." Carolina Biological Supply Company. http://www.carolina.com

Norsworthy, Cheryl B. "The Effects of Selenium on the Death Rate of Brine Shrimp." McPherson College or Science and Technology. http://www.mcpherson.edu

## Chapter Eleven: Relevant Websites

**United Kingdom Websites**:

Blanchard, Clare Elizabeth. "Early Development of the Thorax and the Nervous System of the Brine Shrimp."
<https://lra.le.ac.uk/handle/2381/27631>

"Brine Shrimps." Practical Fishkeeping.
<http://forum.practicalfishkeeping.co.uk/>

"Biology: The Effect of Temperature on Brine Shrimp." Education Scotland.
<http://www.educationscotland.gov.uk/>

## Chapter Eleven: Relevant Websites

## 4.) General Info for Sea Monkeys

In this section you will find a number of sites which contain general information on Sea Monkeys.

**United States Websites:**

"Introduction, Biology and Ecology of Artemia." Fisheries and Aquaculture Department Corporate Document Repository.
<http://www.fao.org/docrep/003/w3732e/w3732e0m.htm>

"Artemia." Animal Diversity Web – University of Michigan Museum of Zoology.
<http://animaldiversity.ummz.umich.edu/ >

"Artemia salina – Brine Shrimp." Encyclopedia of Life.
<http://eol.org/pages/1020243/details>

"Growing Adult Brine Shrimp." Aquatic Community.
<http://www.aquaticcommunity.com/fishfood/growingadultbrineshrimp.php>

Gilbert, Mike. "The Complete Guide to Artemia (Brine Shrimp." SeaHorse.org.
<http://www.seahorse.org/library/articles/artemiaGuide.shtml>

## Chapter Eleven: Relevant Websites

**United Kingdom Websites**:

"Brine Shrimp." Encyclo Online Encyclopedia.
<http://www.encyclo.co.uk/define/brine%20shrimp>

"Nutrition Part 3: Artemia." Reef Ramblings.
<http://reeframblings.co.uk/?page_id=502>

"Tips for the Hatching and Rearing of the Brine Shrimp Artemia." NT Labs. <http://www.ntlabs.co.uk/>

"Artemia and Artemia Breeding." Reptilica.
<http://www.reptilica.co.uk/Artemia_Artemia_breeding.chtml>

"Hatching Brine Shrimp Eggs (Artemia Cysts)." Fish and Fits. <http://www.fishandfits.co.uk/ >

# Index

## *A*

accessories ..................................................................... 11, 33
aeration ............................................................................. 77, 89
air pump ............................................................ 35, 66, 79, 87, 97, 98
algae ..................................................................... 27, 37, 60, 63, 86
ammonia ................................................................. 12, 61, 79, 80
anatomy .......................................................................................... 14
aquarium 9, 11, 12, 15, 18, 24, 32, 33, 34, 35, 37, 38, 39, 41, 42, 43, 46, 48, 50, 53, 54, 57, 59, 78, 79, 80, 86, 93, 102, 117
aquarium fish ................................................................................. 9
aquatic ............................................. 9, 11, 12, 15, 22, 32, 53, 78, 85, 95, 96
Artemia 15, 16, 22, 28, 29, 85, 95, 101, 103, 105, 107, 108, 114, 115, 116, 117, 118

## *B*

bacteria ............................................................. 11, 12, 42, 74, 78, 80
biology ............................................................................................ 14
birth .......................................................................................... 26, 27
breed ................................................................................... 24, 64, 69
breeding ............................................................ 4, 64, 84, 94, 108
brine shrimp 9, 12, 15, 16, 18, 19, 22, 26, 27, 28, 37, 41, 46, 47, 48, 50, 60, 64, 67, 74, 82, 85, 95, 114, 116
buying ................................................................ 30, 33, 35, 46, 50

P a g e | **114**

# C

| | |
|---|---|
| captivity | 61 |
| care | 4, 10, 24, 33, 38, 56, 84, 88, 94, 95, 100, 117 |
| circulation | 35, 41 |
| common mistakes | 88 |
| costs | 33, 37, 38 |
| crustacean | 15, 22, 60, 85, 95 |
| cysts | 19, 46, 47, 75, 89 |

# D

| | |
|---|---|
| dechlorination | 35 |
| decorations | 33, 34, 38, 54 |
| development | 26, 81 |
| diet | 23, 52, 60 |
| diseases | 72, 73, 78, 79 |
| dormant | 19, 22, 25, 47, 70, 85 |

# E

| | |
|---|---|
| eat | 10, 27, 37, 61 |
| eggs | 9, 19, 22, 23, 24, 25, 26, 27, 31, 33, 34, 35, 37, 38, 39, 40, 41, 46, 47, 48, 49, 50, 51, 52, 64, 65, 67, 69, 75, 85, 89, 96, 97 |
| environment | 19, 29, 32, 33, 73, 82, 92 |
| eyes | 18, 22, 85 |

## F

facts .................................................................... 10, 14, 24, 30
feed .................................................................................. 60, 102
feeding ................................ 4, 61, 63, 76, 77, 86, 94, 97, 101, 105, 107
female ............................................................... 16, 19, 22, 69, 85
filter .............................................. 13, 35, 41, 42, 60, 63, 78, 79, 86, 97
food .... 9, 18, 22, 27, 32, 37, 38, 60, 61, 62, 76, 85, 97, 98, 101, 103, 105
freeze-dried ................................................................... 34, 46, 48
frequently asked questions ..................................................... 94

## H

habitat ....................................................................... 29, 52, 53, 60, 84
hatch 19, 22, 23, 31, 35, 37, 39, 40, 41, 46, 47, 51, 64, 67, 70, 71, 75, 76, 85, 89, 96, 97, 118
hatched ............................................................. 12, 23, 26, 27, 50, 67, 98
hatchery ............................................................................. 41, 50, 51
health ..................................................................... 4, 71, 72, 76, 77, 80
healthy ............................................................. 35, 37, 45, 52, 56, 71, 79
heater .................................................................................. 35, 43, 93
hydrometer ................................................................................. 35

## I

initial costs .................................................................................. 33

## L

| | |
|---|---|
| lamp | 35, 43, 67, 87, 92 |
| length | 16 |
| lifespan | 23, 24, 39, 50, 95 |

## M

| | |
|---|---|
| maintain | 11, 35, 43, 56, 79, 81, 83 |
| monthly costs | 33 |

## N

| | |
|---|---|
| nauplii | 18, 60, 67 |
| nitrogen cycle | 11, 12, 80 |
| nutritional needs | 52 |

## O

| | |
|---|---|
| other pets | 23, 30 |
| Overcrowding | 73, 76, 91 |
| overfeeding | 61 |
| oxygen | 19, 41, 57, 58, 81, 89, 98 |

## P

| | |
|---|---|
| parasites | 73, 74 |
| parthenogenesis | 69, 87 |
| pet stores | 46, 51, 80 |
| phytoplankton | 37, 60, 63, 86 |

predators ................................................................. 16, 19
prevent ............................................................................ 79
preventing ...................................................................... 79
pros and cons ......................................................... 39, 50
purchasing ........................................ 31, 43, 46, 48, 49, 50

## Q

questions ................................................... 4, 30, 88, 94

## R

raising ................................................................ 4, 52, 64
relevant websites ...................................................... 100
reproduction ........................................... 18, 19, 25, 69
resources ................................ 100, 101, 103, 105, 107, 117

## S

salinity .............. 15, 18, 22, 32, 35, 53, 58, 62, 73, 78, 83, 85, 92, 96
salt .. 12, 29, 33, 35, 39, 40, 53, 54, 58, 59, 62, 65, 66, 74, 86, 87, 92, 116
saltwater ................. 15, 22, 26, 29, 47, 53, 57, 67, 75, 78, 85, 95, 96
Sea Monkey kit .................................................. 24, 41, 60
shedding ......................................................................... 16
sick ......................................................... 10, 71, 72, 79
space ............................................................ 14, 26, 27, 91, 118
species ........................................ 15, 16, 18, 19, 28, 29, 69, 82, 95
supplier ............................................................... 45, 50
supplies ....................................................................... 38

## T

tank ............ 11, 12, 13, 23, 24, 31, 32, 33, 34, 35, 36, 37, 41, 42, 43, 50, 52, 53, 54, 56, 58, 61, 62, 66, 67, 69, 70, 73, 75, 76, 77, 78, 79, 80, 81, 83, 89, 91, 92, 95, 96, 97, 98, 99
tap water ............ 11, 35, 58, 65, 66, 96
temperature ............ 23, 35, 42, 43, 53, 78, 82, 83, 92, 95, 96, 98
thermometer ............ 35
toxins ............ 35, 56, 95
treatment ............ 72, 74, 78
treatments ............ 72, 74

## W

water changes ............ 56, 78, 79
water purifier ............ 34, 35, 38, 66, 96
water quality ............ 76, 79, 81, 91, 99
width ............ 16

# Photo Credits

Cover image - Derivative (cropped) of Photo By perry-marco via Flickr, titled sea monkey [CC-BY-2.0] (http://creativecommons.org/licenses/by/2.0)], <https://www.flickr.com/photos/zi1217/4825839778/player/8feced02da>

Page 9 Photo By Saul Dolgin (originally posted to Flickr as live brine shrimp) [CC-BY-2.0 (http://creativecommons.org/licenses/by/2.0)], via Wikimedia Commons, <http://commons.wikimedia.org/wiki/File:Live_brine_shrimp.jpg>

Page 15 Photo By Fundacionvallesalado (Own work) [GFDL (http://www.gnu.org/copyleft/fdl.html) or CC-BY-3.0 (http://creativecommons.org/licenses/by/3.0)], via Wikimedia Commons, <http://commons.wikimedia.org/wiki/File:Artemiadeanana.jpg>

Page 16 Photo 18 By Ineuw, via Wikimedia Commons, <http://commons.wikimedia.org/wiki/File:PSM_V04_D218_Artemia_salina.jpg>

Page 27 Photo By Penyulap [CC-BY-SA-3.0 (http://creativecommons.org/licenses/by-sa/3.0)], via Wikimedia Commons, <http://commons.wikimedia.org/wiki/File:15pen.jpg>

Page 30 Photo By Veronidae (Own work) [CC-BY-SA-3.0 (http://creativecommons.org/licenses/by-sa/3.0)], via Wikimedia Commons, <http://commons.wikimedia.org/wiki/File:Artemia_salina_(Linnaeus,_1758)_2013_000.jpg>

Page 31 Photo By Nicolas Joly (1812–1885) [Public domain], via Wikimedia Commons, <http://commons.wikimedia.org/wiki/File:Artemia_salina_painting.png>

Page 47 Photo By Hans Hillewaert via Wikimedia Commons, <http://en.wikipedia.org/wiki/File:Artemia_salina_2.jpg>

Page 52 Photo By AlejandroLinaresGarcia (Own work) [GFDL (http://www.gnu.org/copyleft/fdl.html) or CC-BY-SA-3.0-2.5-2.0-1.0 (http://creativecommons.org/licenses/by-sa/3.0)], via Wikimedia Commons, <http://commons.wikimedia.org/wiki/File:BrineShrimpVeracruz.JPG>

Page 55 Photo purchased from Dreamstime

Page 67 Photo By Hans Hillewaert (Own work) [CC-BY-SA-3.0 (http://creativecommons.org/licenses/by-sa/3.0)], via Wikimedia Commons, <http://commons.wikimedia.org/wiki/File:Artemia_salina_5.jpg>

Page 75 Photo By michelle jo (Own work) [CC-BY-3.0 (http://creativecommons.org/licenses/by/3.0)], via Wikimedia Commons, <http://commons.wikimedia.org/wiki/File:Many_live_brine_shrimp.JPG>

Page 89 Photo By Neil Phillips from uk (Turda salt marsh - brine shrimp) [CC-BY-2.0 (http://creativecommons.org/licenses/by/2.0)], via Wikimedia Commons,

<http://commons.wikimedia.org/wiki/File:Turda_salt_marsh_-_brine_shrimp.jpg>

Page 93 Photo By DJMapleFerryman via Wikimedia Commons,
<http://en.wikipedia.org/wiki/File:Artemia_monica.jpg>

Page 99 Photo By Adrianer, via Wikimedia Commons,
<http://commons.wikimedia.org/wiki/File:Artemia_salina.jpg>

Page 105 Photo By Hans Hillewaert via Wikimedia Commons,
<http://en.wikipedia.org/wiki/File:Artemia_salina_4.jpg>

# References

"Artemia." Animal Diversity Web – University of Michigan Museum of Zoology. <http://animaldiversity.ummz.umich.edu/accounts/Artemia/classification/>

"Artemia salina – Brine Shrimp." Encyclopedia of Life. <http://eol.org/pages/1020243/details>

"Brine Shrimp." Carolina Biological Supply Company. <http://www.carolina.com/teacher-resources/Document/brine-shrimp-care-handling/tr10481.tr>

"Common Water Quality Issues & Remedies." Drs. Foster and Smith. <http://www.liveaquaria.com/PIC/article.cfm?aid=220>

"Discovering Brine Shrimp and their Parasites." Utah Education Network. <http://www.uen.org>

Emslie, Sara. "Artemia salina." Animal Diversity Web, University of Michigan Museum of Zoology. <http://animaldiversity.ummz.umich.edu/accounts/Artemia_salina/>

"Glossary of Aquarium Terms." LiveAquaria.com. <http://www.liveaquaria.com/PIC/article.cfm?aid=243>

"Glossary of Aquarium Terms." Sea and Sky. <http://www.seasky.org/aquarium/aquarium-glossary.html>

"Introduction, Biology and Ecology of Artemia." Fisheries and Aquaculture Department Corporate Document Repository. <http://www.fao.org/docrep/003/w3732e/w3732e0m.htm>

"Nitrogen Cycle and Aquarium & Pond Cycling." American Aquarium. <http://www.americanaquariumproducts.com/nitrogen_cycle.html>

"Science Watch; Shrimp Hatch in Space." The New York Times. <http://www.nytimes.com/1991/05/14/science/science-watch-shrimp-hatch-in-space.html>

Solangi, Mobashir A., et al. "A Filamentous Bacterium on the Brine Shrimp and its Control." University of Nebraska – Lincoln. <http://digitalcommons.unl.edu/parasitologyfacpubs/490/>

Spooner, Brian S., et al. "Brine Shrimp Development in Space: Ground-Based Data to Shuttle Flight Results." Transactions of the Kansas Academy of Science. 95 (1-2), 1992. Pp. 87-92.

"Tips for the Hatching and Rearing of the Brine Shrimp Artemia." NT Labs. <http://www.ntlabs.co.uk/learning-zone/28/Aquarium+-+Brine+Shrimp+Hatching+Tips>

"What are the Guidelines for Culturing Brine Shrimp?" Brine Shrimp Direct. <http://www.brineshrimpdirect.com/what-are-the-guidelines-for-culturing-brine-shrimp-c119.html>

CPSIA information can be obtained
at www.ICGtesting.com
Printed in the USA
BVOW06s0253181217
503092BV00023B/2532/P